Fides Qua Creditur

CAN I LIVE BETTER

Franny Hill

authorHOUSE®

AuthorHouse™
1663 Liberty Drive
Bloomington, IN 47403
www.authorhouse.com
Phone: 1-800-839-8640

Published by AuthorHouse   11/04/2014

ISBN: 978-1-4969-5091-8 (sc)
ISBN: 978-1-4969-5090-1 (e)

Contents

✓

"We were not made to avoid responsibility; it is the vehicle by which we experience fulfillment in our lives. There is where we have commonality."

Hosea 14:9 (KJV)

✓

Our Focus: Let us be found to be deserving of our place within HIS kingdom. Make no mistake: salvation is our responsibility.

✓

"We are the inheritance of wisdom. It shall become a part of us like a dear friend. This gift shall never go astray."

Matthew 11:19 (KJV)

✓

Our Focus: For us, there is but one choice. Wisdom will make us whole, for it comes from above. Let your consciousness take you to the truth.

✓

"The human mind is barraged by information that; diminishes the hope we have attained. However, hope burns eternal for those who nurture their spirit."

Lamentations 3:26 (KJV)

✓

Our Focus: When we consider what we have survived, let there be hope. The world is on the verge of something remarkable.

✓

"Lamentations 3:26 says, "It is good that a man should both hope and quietly wait for salvation of the LORD." To have a home is the manifestation of our hopes. Welcome home."

Lamentations 3:26 (KJV)

✓

Our focus: There is hope for us all. That hope has no pre-requisites. Continue on your journey allowing hope to be your guide.

✓

"We are born makers, more precisely, in the image of GOD. We can earn almost anything except-salvation. Take some time and ask for the ability to forgive others. Then, let that same forgiveness be bestowed upon you."

Ephesians 4:28 (KJV)

✓

Our Focus: The spirit embodies our understanding of right and wrong. Working for our sustenance gives us the freedom to help those who cannot.

✓

"On the average we take our health for granted. Unintentionally, we expect it to just be there like a favorite item at the convenience store. Today, we can make some better decisions to maintain our health. Let us make use of our common sense for more than just opinions."

Proverbs 12:18 (KJV)

✓

Our Focus: The tongue of the wise can make healthy those who are sick. We need to maintain our condition for living. It will give us the years we desire most of all.

✓

"Love cannot be secured through a contract. If you want love then, you must produce love. The way to feel love is to give love. What you put into a relationship you will get out of that situation."

Matthew 5:44 (KJV)

✓

Our Focus: We intuitively are intuitively drawn to the ones closest to us. We ought to let love push us towards others who may be a source of doubt for us.

Introspection: Week 1

The only sure thing in life is a beginning and an ending. Fill your space with all the pieces of your puzzle. Then, allow the human attraction to assemble the view. Make room in your life for those who feel neglected. Amends is the way to a brighter future.

✓

"Our role in society is sometimes a reflection of our role at home. It can be said that the opposite is true too. Carry yourself with dignity and self-respect."

1 Peter 1:18 (KJV)

✓

Our Focus: Some of the things that matter most to us come by traditions. Historically, our fathers are the source of family traditions. Our mothers help to strengthen such traditional values.

✓

"We need not worry over a lack of zeal in our lives. For zeal, comes over time and effort. Therefore, labor not in a hurry- labor with patience and consistency."

Isaiah 9:7 (KJV)

✓

Our Focus: We must focus our concern on completing the assignment without hindering the results. This will increase our passion for the work. After all is said and done we will see that we are not in charge of the results. Our job is to do the work.

✓

"We can put an emphasis on wealth but, no two people see wealth the same way. There may be some who feel like they deserve more than the next person. I imagine that singles and couples will have different reasons to acquire more of it."

Psalm 49:6 (KJV)

✓

Our Focus: Resist the temptation to glorify your affluence. With grace, you may pay it forward to someone in need, including someone you know. "A friend in need is a friend in deed" is what my dad told me.

✓

"The world is not troubled by weather however; whether you seek forgiveness could trouble your world. Try to be more forgiving and you will be forgiven more. The way you treat others is the way others will treat you. Do not rely solely on your own ideas. My professor told me, 'Shake a hand make a friend.' The answers are inside you."

MATTHEW 26:28 (KJV)

✓

Our Focus: We were bound to address it, the need for forgiveness, in this conversation. The remission of sins is our ultimate quest of the spirit. We want to someday rest in unity with our GOD.

✓

"We gain much of our resources without offering much gratitude. The amends is obvious to all who can see. The cycle must be broken. Poverty is an attitude not just a condition. Some who claim poverty is not poor they make others poor. It is a vicious cycle that corrodes the morale of a society."

Psalm 19:11 (KJV)

✓

Our Focus: Make a resolution and a decision to do something nice for someone for no reason. Let the thought be your reward. Giving should come from the heart.

✓

"Have there been any calamities that were averted? Was it through a belief in a power not of your own? There are miracles experienced by many daily. Some things cannot be explained away yet, we call it Providence. Simply, look into the eyes of one who has survived such an incident and there you will see the source of such power."

Psalm 127:3 (KJV)

✓

Our Focus: We may ask ourselves about what we deserve then, more importantly, we can examine what we think we deserve. Your way is not always the best way.

✓

"The life we lead will eventually require us to sacrifice something for something else. These situations demand that we have prior experience with give-and-take. The "willing power" will be there all we need to do is call on it. By humbling ourselves we receive access to that power as a source of guidance for our decision."

Romans 8:28 (KJV)

✓

Our Focus: You may assess your community structure. I will assess my environment. There can be similarities that do not fade in the disparaging over our differences.

Introspection: Week 2

Considering the challenges of our daily affairs, let us give time for the ones that yield the most fulfillments. There is a chance you will discover your own inclinations to contribute. Give yourself more to life and life will give more to you.

✓

"Does it ever feel like too much is being asked of you? How do we complete all of our tasks in order to feel a sense of accomplishment? That answer most likely will vary from one person to the next. What we need to remember is that we like everyone else have our limits. Trying to do it all at once will only make us feel overwhelmed. There is always a now then a later."

Psalm 18:32 (KJV)

✓

Our focus: Historically, weight has been associated with strength. Today, we know that size is not an indicator of strength. We want the strength but not the weight. Stay in alignment with your weight training goals. Big and strong is not what it seems.

✓

"We do not have to choose brains or brawn. Yet a wise man once said, "I will take brains over brawn any day." That wise man was my father (RIP). To live a victorious life; train your brain like you train your brawn."

Ecclesiastes 9:16 (KJV)

✓

Our Focus: One of the least admired attributes is brains. Our brains achieve so much more than muscle on a daily basis. It would be hard for us to accomplish much without it. Respect yourself by guarding your brain, for the body is only an extension of it.

✓

"There are some of us who claim to have been called by GOD. Still others say HE touched me. I do not wander anymore how I can earn the favor of GOD. My faith is what matters for a touch may not be the way to heaven but merely a sign I need help. I like you have lived long enough to know that it is different for everyone-Amazing Grace."

Philippians 3:6 (KJV)

✓

Our Focus: We make life a struggle when we over analyze internal circumstances. Use your connection to the "willing power" to gain understanding and peace.

✓

"The "willing power" is generous in caring for our lives. We have free will that allows us to accept that care every day. Do not edge GOD out by your pride or the illusion of total self- sufficiency. With its presence we can tolerate some level of ambiguity."

Job 28:28 (KJV)

✓

Our Focus: We would do better adopting awareness and a respect for the power greater than ourselves. This is the same power that is always with us-just acknowledge it.

✓

"We hustle through life with our feelers out for the best paying job or the most lucrative contract and let's not forget that grand commission. What could be better than money – try getting some knowledge?"

Proverbs 16:16 (KJV)

✓

Our focus: Money will take us only so far. However, a spiritual understanding will help us overcome any obstacle. We will rise above any trap or distraction that could take us off course.

✓

"My life was in a dead end before I began to love others. It began with my family and friends. Then, I started to feel more love than I could give. Tradition taught me when to shake hands for my father was an advocate for the right manners at the right time."

2 Thessalonians 2:15 (KJV)

✓

Our Focus: Each one of us is responsible for the children we serve. Be cautious of what you teach them outside the classroom.

✓

"Today is the start of something wonderful. There may be a cure discovered for cancer or Alzheimer's. Anything is possible we must believe in miracles. It is a shame we cannot put GOD down on our resumes for a reference."

Psalm 27:9 (KJV)

✓

Our Focus: When we reach out to someone we know, to be of service, the road we are on gets a little wider. We can always use some more space. Cool

Introspection: Week 3

There is certain energy in the midst of the groups we are members of. Let your spirit become a source to that energy. Make the sharing effectual.

✓

"We may have often wondered how to get spiritual. Or, do we have any spirituality? It may have surprised us when were told that perfection s not spirituality. For many of us that was the idea that kept us looking for it in all the wrong places. It was such a relief to know that; we could attain a level of spirituality just as we were."

Psalm 51:10 (KJV)

✓

Our focus: We need not dismiss ourselves from life due to our imperfections. Concentrate on what we have and allow Providence to take care of our shortcomings.

✓

"It has been said that humility will open doors for us that were closed. Humility comes from the awareness of our own deficits in our character. We do not have to limit ourselves to frustration and dissatisfaction. Let us move beyond this point on the promises of the Creator who made us all."

Genesis 6:3 (KJV)

✓

Our focus: At this point we can make adjustments to our character. However, we must pursue excellence while relinquishing the desire for perfection.

✓

"There is more to life than the pursuit of material desires. Opening ourselves to a more intimate connection to nature will probably spark interest in more intangible experiences. Let us make our days count then, we can count our days."

Revelations 22:14 (KJV)

✓

Our Focus: We want to be compensated for being of service. Count your blessings while we make the world a little warmer for someone in need.

✓

"Every day we try to live as a community. We do the best we can to take care of each other. There are things we do for our neighbors, families, friends, and coworkers that really say, "I got your back." These actions find their origin in a spirit within our community. Let us honor such a spirit."

Luke 1:77 (KJV)

Our focus: All of our needs will not be met when we try to go it alone. Grab a seat with some of us and we can show you how it works.

✓

"People are tempted to do wrong. That means us too. The only thing that we can do is hope to make the amends for our shortsightedness. Most people will understand. Try not to be superior or inferior to anyone. Loneliness can be very frightening."

Colossians 2:18 (KJV)

✓

Our focus: we all desire security. The best security is experience. We will have our own yet, at times, we can learn from others. How great is that?

I want what is coming…   January 27

✓

"As children we spent many hours scheming ways to get what we wanted. Working for it was as unattractive as a, Friday night home with the parents. As we grew older we saw that most people earned what they have. It was not just given to them. Today, we see things differently."

1 Timothy 5:18 (KJV)

✓

Our Focus: We feel good when people acknowledge our efforts to support ourselves. Let your gratitude show for what you have. No one else can do it but you.

✓

"Whatever is your primary goal requires you to make choices that may alter the course of your life. We must be willing to endure failure as much as we crave success. Some of our most celebrated achievers are our worst losers- 'Abraham Lincoln' is case in point. He lost the race for the presidency more than once. Keep trying."

Matthew 5:12 (KJV)

✓

Our Focus: What we need to understand about making plans is that we make the plans, not the results.

Introspection: Week 4

Striving for the good life is no guarantee that we will live better. Pause for a moment, then, ask yourself where does it end? We are more in tune with what really matters. For me it was family and friends. I am living in the good life.

✓

"On any given day we can hav3e disagreements. In fact, they can be downright hostile. The situation can be diffused when both parties recoil at "being right" in order, to allow all to be heard. No one is more important than any other."

Proverbs 21:2 (KJV)

✓

Our Focus: We all have made mistakes we would like to undo. The goal is to not make the same mistakes again and again. Try something different.

✓

"There are things that money cannot buy. There are feelings poverty does not give. At either extreme we want something. If we can just think about what we need we will be happy with what we get. It is all in the attitude."

Proverbs 30:8 (KJV)

✓

Our Focus: Today our greatest task is to treat others like we want to be treated. There is no grieving a challenge than to play by the rules when you see others are not.

✓

"How long was it before we claimed such a bond? For some of us we said it in high school, others said it at prayer night, and still others whispered it at break time. Remember that day chances are there was someone else listening."

John 13:34 (KJV)

✓

Our Focus: It is with great joy we engage in love for it makes us feel whole. Therefore, be ready to share your love with others. Give it away and when it returns it is yours.

✓

"We have all been caught off guard at times. It can be embarrassing. It would be wise to practice prevention concerning such things as safety issues. We cannot afford to let anything compromise our knowledge of what is right. It just may save some lives."

Galatians 3:5 (KJV)

✓

Our Focus: The world needs people like us who care about how they treat it. Take care of yourself; together, we can care for her.

✓

"Did the alarm clock wake you up today? Then, take it out to the closest cemetery and set it off. Count how many people get up to answer it. We take such occasions like this for granted. However, some people who were not in the final resting place were unable to answer that alarm clock as well."

Acts 2:22 (KJV)

✓

Our focus: we are becoming accustomed to the misuse of our own resources. Make a difference by contributing to the whole community without taking. Preservation is key to longevity.

✓

"There are many worthwhile careers society offers. We are told to find one that best suits our culture and goals. I have a somewhat different philosophy. Look for your niche- it may not be what you want but; the payoff could be great. In addition, you may make someone very proud."

Acts 8:20 (KJV)

✓

Our Focus: Money is not the answer for everything. Our love for it devalues life. It is time to look inside ourselves to discover what we really want. What is our passion in life?

✓

"Life is a place where we are given many stimuli. Some of the time we respond more appropriately than others. Let your life be an exercise in nurturing the mind by sending it good thoughts. In time we can learn how to bridge the gap between thought and intention."

Isaiah 55:1 (KJV)

✓

Our Focus: We ought to be kind to our neighbor; for one day, they may be our greatest hope.

✓

"There is a particular phrase that comes to mind. Here and now let us think outside any moral confines. Look at the practical application on a daily basis. It is not birth that keeps the world going but mercy."

Hebrews 4:16 (KJV)

✓

Our Focus: Today, we thank the "Willing Power" for all it has done for us - AWESOME.

<u>All for one and one for all</u>

✓

"We know that not so long ago the unthinkable happened. Now we are flooded with threats against our way of life on every coast. There are graphic and profane demonstrations of hatred towards us. We should not just be afraid but empathetic towards our critics. We should choose our mood not someone in a homemade video."

John 15:13 (KJV)

✓

Our Focus: There is nothing that can separate us from the care of GOD.

✓

"My goal in life was to be successful just like yours. How do we measure success? Is it in materialism or is it intangible? Material success is not the end for everyone. However, wielding it is an intangible talent. We should all be able to go home and feel like our lives matter."

Psalm 91:16 (KJV)

✓

Our Focus: All hope rest on the foundation that someone besides us will benefit from our act of faith (Fides Qua Creditur)

Introspection: Week 5

Your light may shine but; does anyone see it. Live today not only for yourself and remember, you are not alone. Take a pause – in memory or reflection of someone who cares for you.

✓

"How many times have we heard someone tell us that we analyze things too much? Are we sticklers for the details? Maybe we think we know more than anyone else. We could discover that; what we think we know is only for us to know. In such case, modesty is the best policy. We do not want to be overwhelming."

John 6:35 (KJV)

✓

Our focus: Good health is a necessity to live a productive life. However, the standards are not etched in stone. Less thought more action in your community. Your efforts count. Nice

✓

"Today we have the opportunity to do what no other people can do. The opportunities are endless. The progress has been achieving new heights. Let us help each other like we were helped. The spirit of service to our fellow human beings gives us much to look forward to. Remember, no man is an island."

1 Corinthians 15:19 (KJV)

✓

Our Focus: We must make our own beds. The work is done before the reward and after. Settle down. You have to be in for the long haul. Anything worth having requires effort.

✓

"What have we done to our children? It cost more to raise a child then to buy a home. Children are our greatest gift that; we have to look forward to. Let us not deny them the gift of hope for it was given to us. Our greatest work is how we pass that blessing on to them."

Ephesians 5:8 (KJV)

✓

Our Focus: Pray – Meditate – Study. It is the new PMS. Anyone can participate including our children.

✓

"Psalm 119:105 says, "Thy word is a Lamp onto my feet, and a light unto my path." We have great meaning in the reverence we offer Him. Do not be ashamed of your God-capacity, for to know Him is to love HIM."

Psalm 119:105 (KJV)

✓

Our Focus: GOD can do great things with us without our permission. Great works are in HIS hands.

✓

"In the world of a criminal, life is a tool to get what you want or needed. There are priorities however; they are not like every day priorities. When you're in it – forever is the creed. Hold your head up and shout for, there but for the grace of GOD go me."

John 3:36 (KJV)

✓

Our Focus: Make a commitment to obey your parents, your people, and your guardians. And yes, they want to save you. Should you doubt their words, turn it over to the Creator.

✓

"The process of aging is one of the most feared aspects of our lives. We try to control it or alter the effects. Truth is we have as much power over that as we do the temperature of the sun. Let's try to flow with it and allow the ebb of life to work things out."

Psalm 19:2 (KJV)

✓

Our Focus: We experience many feelings during the course of the day. It has an effect on our mind and mood. The effects can be a sign that we can make it through the day.

✓

"For now we have made a tradition for others to follow. The pursuit of happiness is guaranteed. However, it does not promise us we will achieve that elusive feeling. Each one of us must design happiness for ourselves."

2 Peter 3:18 (KJV)

✓

Our Focus: we will have life more abundantly when we surrender our will to HIM.

Introspection: Week 6

The spiritual life is built on a foundation. Perhaps, simplicity is the strongest form of honesty. Just because something is simple does not mean it is easy. Have faith for the path goes through not around.

✓

"We are told that charity begins at home. We should apply that principle to all things that are right. How we teach our loved ones is how they will teach others as they mature. Our duty is to provide them with the right information."

1 Corinthians 13:13 (KJV)

✓

Our Focus: We all want to feel safe again. One way to accomplish such a task is to attend to the needy here at home. We need to do more than just pray this demands that we develop a real plan for relief here and now.

✓

"When we remove our own selfish agendas there is a higher calling we try to adhere to. It takes practice to know when to stay quiet. Yes, we can have the things we want however, in acquiring those things do we cause harm. Sometimes what we want the most can cause the most damage."

Romans 5:4 (KJV)

✓

Our Focus: When we think only of ourselves we do ourselves a disservice. Try to demonstrate some consideration for others. It may just make your day.

✓

"All of us have received the hope of tomorrow yet; have any of us ever seen a tomorrow? When someone makes me a promise I ask myself, can I do it myself? The answer does not lessen the hope instead of feeling indifferent; my hope grows to a point of being transferable. That means I can share that hope best by returning the good deed that was done for me."

Proverbs 16:19 (KJV)

✓

Our Focus: Be yourself, for there are many good things that can be achieved when you are being you. In fact, no one else can do that – be yourself.

✓

"One day we may find the way to end hunger. Today, we can share a meal or even spring for one. It will make us feel better yet, the solution to some problems is repetition. Buy a meal each day for a needy person who is unable to. Do not doubt there is more we can do. We can help even from the comfort of our luxurious home."

Psalm 9:12 (KJV)

✓

Our Focus: In the midst of the storm, many were doing all they could to save those in need. When we ban together there is no storm that can dampen our faith.

✓

"Be cheerfully ready to go the extra mile, give some extra change, stay that extra day, these are the measures that flow from the heart. We can have all the time in the world to do something different. However, the change in us comes from our willingness. If you need some it is time to hit your knees. Think of all the binds HE got you out of the next, take stock of the times you have had your way with someone."

Acts 20:19 (KJV)

✓

Our Focus: All we have to do is ask and we shall receive.

✓

"The prognosis is dismal the pain growing, the meaning of life lost. A final good-bye can be very painful yet; it happens every day, everywhere, every time. Let the time you had with them be your heirloom to save. We will be able to say we tried for all we cared about."

Titus 2:13 (KJV)

✓

Our Focus: We must surely try to live our best each day. Living our best means we try to contribute to society. There is no remorse in serving, for it is an aspiration of the human heart.

✓

"In the academic world or academia, there is a shortage of discipline. We cram for finals, ask for cheat sheets, demand open book test and request sample test questions. Make the time to study, go ahead; think of it as an investment in your parents' future. There will be less sleepless nights and more praise for you. Also, you will be the shining example for your younger sibling. Hurray!!!"

Proverbs 3:13 (KJV)

✓

Our focus: Learning is not for anyone, but it is for those who use it.

Introspection: Week 7

We have the greatest capacity for learning when we combine it with service. Make decisions that solidify your opportunities then; look for ways to be of service. You will go further than you imagine.

✓

"We have so much to be grateful for. Do not allow the unknown to dictate your mood or your thoughts. Every day there is something to get out of bed for. The way we live is an indication of how we think. There is no other country that bestows upon its citizens the liberties as we have it. Everyone deserves to feel like they have it good. We have our differences yet, there is more we share in common than what we do not. You are responsible for your own happiness."

1 Peter 3:4 (KJV)

✓

Our Focus: Today, give something you like to a friend for keeps. Take notice of their reaction. You may have just made their day. Our favorite things are best when they are shared.

✓

"We could not wait any longer. Everyone wanted more than what I could offer. So, I turned inward and I was in awe of the landscape. There were skills just sitting there waiting to be tapped. Subsequently, we found ourselves here. This project is not just about me. My family has been very supportive and encouraging. Get your family involved with some of your projects as it may inspire you by what they say. Sometimes we must tell them – keep the job, thanks but no thanks."

Joshua 8:1 (KJV)

✓

Our Focus: No one can treat me better as their employee but me. Therefore, I hired myself without an application, resume, or referral. Now, I can say it is my money. (LOL) Cool

✓

"We must set the bar high enough to challenge ourselves. There may be a lot we don't know yet. It will also separate the top grade from the less qualified grade. We will keep preparing each day for our lives. When you plan to succeed you plan to live. Let no one be a distraction from your abilities to conquer. Together, we can achieve more than we can apart."

Luke 12:32 (KJV)

✓

Our Focus: We will not be slaves to fear. We will only conquer it, then tell the good news.

✓

"And now there is more responsibility we can share. Let your conscious guide your decision. There are times that we must work with others yet, the work must be done. If you have to pick up the slack that; will affect your performance. If you are truly disciplined then, there will be no disturbance to the work. A team will either succeed together or fall apart at the seams into failure. Do your best to make your team a winner."

Haggai 2:7 (KJV)

✓

Our Focus: Let us make our path the one less traveled, by leading through example. The time for talking is over. Success demands action. Give your all to the cause. Make your own conscience feel good about what you have done.

✓

"Our best efforts have changed the course of our lives. Now, we need to invite a "Willing Power" into our life to show us what we still need to learn. In fact, we may be called on to teach a family member what we have just learned. The Power will help us navigate the vessel through the murky depth of our character."

Isaiah 26:8 (KJV)

✓

Our Focus: Do not be confused. The test of our stability will come in how we respond to the trials of life. There is much to share when we come into the light. Be willing to receive the light; then, you will want to share it.

✓

"The quality of our health depends not just on how we eat. Our daily routine may be depleting our health. We must be ready to change and try something new. We discard what does not work and hold onto what does. Yes, we can have golden years when life is meant to be sweeter than honey itself. Take charge of your health."

Romans 8:17 (KJV)

✓

Our Focus: Be mindful of your surroundings. Keep a clean house, for it signifies peace of mind. Your health will stay good when you are active at home as you are outside. Home is where we find that peace we seek.

✓

"Here and now we must give back to the source of all that is good. Our families are the biggest source of encouragement. We have heard how it does the mind good to share our resources. Be a cheerful giver and the reward will exceed any expectation. Our part of being blessed is to receive but, first we must learn how to give for there is no greater duty than too share with others."

Hebrews 13:8 (KJV)

✓

Our Focus: Be humble enough to accept the truths. Then, you do not have to be forced. There is great wisdom when you know when to speak and how to listen. You will reveal the truth in both places.

Introspection: Week 8

There have been a lot of negative reports about America and our sitting President. Do your part to make this and keep this the greatest country in the world. Together we can rebuke the naysayers, and then, wave our flags for all to see.

✓

"Today we have the opportunity to do what no other people can do. The gifts are endless. Let us help each other as we were helped. There is no man who is an island. We must ask for help because, people cannot read our minds. You have to unharden your heart to allow the joy of community into your life."

1 Corinthians 15:19 (KJV)

✓

Our Focus: We must make our own fortune. Everyone is not going to be rich, yet, there is a possibility that all can be happy. There is no reward without the work. Buckle up: you're in for a long ride.

✓

"When we receive information our need for accuracy is not always evident. We tend to exercise a level of skepticism. However, when relaying information we want to believe we are always right. Remain flexible and what you give will be as good as what you get."

Matthew 10:41 (KJV)

✓

Our Focus: Our lives should have a certain amount of continuity. To achieve this continuity we must balance our lives. Then, you will understand how to maintain your flow in life.

✓

"Integrity means to be without impurity, honesty, and uprightness. It can be an elusive quality to emulate yet; we are impressed or even aroused by those who demonstrate it in their lives. Most people are doing their best to remain grounded in principle and show compassion for those who lack that certain something others seem to possess. Such a statement itself is one made with – integrity."

1 Corinthians 3:8 (KJV)

✓

Our Focus: When we attend a social event, make sure our companion is aware of the purpose of the affair. Counterfeit emotions can dampen the enthusiasm. Nice

✓

"Sometimes others have a better perspective than our own. A situation can make us more inclined to anger than compassion. When such a one as mentioned arises, you may need to wait until; you have less ambiguity to cope with it properly. We can become emotionally attached to the situation rendering us incapable of being open- minded."

Hosea 14:9 (KJV)

✓

Our focus: Loved ones can make us emotionally dependent. In our personal relationships it is referred to as codependency. My ex-wife informed me of the stage that describes where we were after our break-up. Free yourself!!!

✓

"Some of us had very memorable high school experiences. For those who feel they missed out, let today be your homecoming. We are glad you are here. Let your conscious be your guide by giving your cares over to Providence. Surely, by now, you know that you are not a mistake. Congratulations are in order for you have made it back to see just how far you have come. CONGRATULATIONS!!!"

Psalm 96:6 (KJV)

✓

Our Focus: We have matured to show kindness to those we once shunned. Do not be turned off by our differences. Instead of intolerance, use this moment to share yourself with one another. Make a cultural connection so that our connection can overcome differences of our cultures.

✓

"This refrain some of have heard from people who know us many times. It was just in fun for most of our lives. Now, we are older and it has become a personal question we have asked ourselves. Emulation is not the highest form of flattery. It only requires a heartfelt thank you to show respect. When you want to feel secure in your manhood, be more attuned to the subtler tones of behavior that make the difference. Good manners have never failed me."

Revelation 5:12 (KJV)

✓

Our Focus: We all have talents. Let those talents be the benchmark of our character.

✓

'Sometimes failures can shake our very foundation of what we know and believe in. However, letting our failures rule our lives is nonsense. I say, "Let your shortcomings be the bridge to success." Nothing beats a failure but a try. You would be hard pressed to sit in self-pity when you have given your all to whatever the challenge was for today. You can be satisfied or not but, the effort is all yours. Go get em."

Exodus 15:2 (KJV)

Our Focus: For whatever reason we all are asked to do the best we can at whatever our occupation. Today, meet that objective and you will have had a good day. I cannot imagine it getting any better than that.

"Our families have been raised with some very important traditions. In our families, the eldest of the generation was responsible for holiday seating arrangements. The purpose was to show each child that they had a place in the family. My family was made up of two families. We still keep this tradition today even though, we are miles apart. However, the two families are together separately. The seating has changed but, the love is still the same. It keeps us young."

2 Thessalonians 3:6 (KJV)

Our Focus: Let us make good use of the many lessons found in family traditions. It could be just what we need to keep our children happy.

Introspection: Week 9

When our accomplishments do not impress us, we need to contemplate on where the strength comes from to meet challenges. In that vein we should have nothing but gratitude. Remember, we are but a small piece of the puzzle.

✓

"Today we are more meticulous with the welfare of our children. We want them to look and feel their best. Managing their lives is sometimes frustrating however; we knew there were no instructions. It requires a lot of time and effort. You can draw strength from the "Willing Power" to get you through the day. Pause, and then get something to sip on and relax. Things are about to change."

Psalm 28:7 (KJV)

✓

Our Focus: A major part of the task is to be present. In time they will let you in for that is what they hope you want. Our children expect us to be our best at all times.

✓

"Once we have made a good first impression our chances for success increase dramatically. Stay focused on your priorities. And believe; we all have them. Two of mine are taking my medicines and making sure I powerwalk three times a week. This makes not just good health but good healthy thoughts as well."

Luke 1:51 (KJV)

✓

Our Focus: we can do more when we have attended to our chores. Do not become a procrastinator. Get it done, whatever it is - you will feel better.

✓

"A friend of mine from the Philippines once referred to a neighbor as ninety-nine. That sounded like an odd description. He hails from Dawau, a small southern town in the Philippines. He told me that; in Dawua, when a person is considered crazy they call them a ninety-nine. In translation it means, they are ninety-nine short of a hundred. Here we would say, "They are not dealing with a full deck (LOL). Yes, however, stigma can be harmful and mean."

Psalm 46:1 (KJV)

✓

Our Focus: As a community we ought to adopt a more proactive stance on fighting stigma. Everyone wants acceptance and it is such a basic human need sort of like traveling...

✓

"2 Corinthians 12:9 says, "… My grace is sufficient for thee: for my strength is made perfect in weakness." There is power in the word for it can make the mind new. Brain cells may not restore themselves but; the word restores those who restore themselves to the word."

2 Corinthians 12:9 (KJV)

✓

Our Focus: If you do have a belief, be true to yourself. No one is impressed by it more than you. Make it a part of your focus.

✓

"Today there is much temptation. People who do not belong in jail are spending years of their lives there because they succumbed to temptation. Do not think that it could not happen to you. We all have less attractive parts of our personalities that it plays on. If we are not careful; we will to be waiting for commissary. Ask yourself this question, "Can I surrender to win?"

Ephesians 1:3 (KJV)

✓

Our Focus: Maturity happens at different times for all of us. Once you know better you must do better.

✓

"Every day we live right helps us to live better. Strive for consistency for with it miracles happen. We can control our fate by letting fate not control us."

Proverbs 24:5 (KJV)

✓

Our Focus: Be the best individual you can by being a number of those that are making things change. Do not give up your birth right.

✓

"We have had to tell a restless teenager that command many times. I would like to believe that they are glad we gave them such attention. Their socialization should not be left to chance. They are our future leaders and makers therefore; we must instill in them the desire for excellence."

Joel 3:10 (KJV)

✓

Our Focus: The children are our first priority. Spare no expense as it pertains to their academic performance. These children will become successes in their own right.

Introspection: Week 10

We would do well to make the most of each day we live our better life. None of the good things we cherish come with a guarantee. We are responsible for our own happiness. There is no more "passing the buck".

✓

"Every day we face obstacles in our lives but, so do our children. We hope that there is a Providence in these situations that; will guide us to the best decision. We doubt that there is any affect in our lives yet; we continue to hope. We must be fair and unyielding to the circumstances that oppose our will. It is Providence that has made the way possible."

Isaiah 35:4 (KJV)

✓

Our Focus: We are the passenger in our lives. Notwithstanding, we still have our need to be behind the wheel. Cool

✓

"I am in the process of pursuing my dreams to be a professional mental health consumer peer advocate. There have been some who wanted to derail my life yet; I did not let resentment distract me from my goals. I received awards and honors from my educators and my colleagues. I continued to satisfy my obligations inherent in my chosen field of study. Stay the course and resist indulgences – be a winner!!!"

Psalm 248 (KJV)

✓

Our Focus: We are on the verge of a major change in the way we handle stressors. This change is possible by the flow of better information and more accurate data. Keep in touch.

✓

"There is a difference in being your worst critic and critical thinking. One could lead to a richer more satisfying life. The other will enrich every decision you make. I would say successful people have a proportionate amount of both. They know when to tell themselves enough is enough. However, they can also correct themselves when it comes to their discipline. Otherwise, life would be flat and fragmented for most of us. Therefore, choose wisely which you will rely on."

Job 12:13(KJV)

✓

Our Focus: Making better choices come from the constant effort to do the right thing. Do not be wishy-washy in your decision making processes.

✓

"When we are at home, feeling safe is priority. Some of us have security systems, or pets, or neighborhood watch. These measures make us feel smart and safe. We have got a leg up on the criminals. However, real security is in the way the home is managed from the inside. Respect and humility will protect your home just as good."

Proverbs 3:5 (KJV)

✓

Our Focus: treat yourself the way you want to be treated. Be good to yourself as well as to others.

✓

"For us there are many opinions about what is truth. The truth is not the same for everybody. It has been said that one man's junk is another man's treasure. Often people will disagree with me yet; I am still able to get to the point. That is what I desire most to be heard for acceptance comes later. I look inward for my validation. I have learned that I will not always be right but right is always inside.

Proverbs 16:22 (KJV)

✓

Our Focus: There may come a day when being right is not as important as being willing. Only Providence controls such a day. Let your faith guide you when there is no one else.

✓

"We aspire to live the good life for it appears attractive to us. We see nice things, good food, fine clothes, and a surplus of cash. However, pleasure requires we have the capacity to feel pain, not misery but; pain. How we react to that pain will determine the life we lead. Can we really tolerate having more than what we need or want. If you don't know you better ask someone."

Psalm 147:5 (KJV)

✓

Our Focus: Make every effort to remain self-supporting. It is a gift that comes through sacrifice and patience. Live your best life now.

✓

"We are fortunate for we are taught behaviors that are acceptable. For me things were clearer when I was younger. Being an adult is unfamiliar territory. I was determined as a child to stay out of hell. Then, I was told I could not do it on my own. I thought I died and went to hell. (LOL) There is nothing more inspiring than a young person wanting to serve GOD. We need to encourage those who are inclined to serve to chase their goals. It is not ambitious but defies ambition."

Isaiah 6:5 (KJV)

✓

Our Focus: Being a person who is confident about his spiritual foundations suggest there is some vulnerability. In what I believe would have it no other way, for where I need HIM the most is where HE meets me.

Introspection: Week 11

When we put an overemphasis on our desires we create a vacuum that we are unable to fill. If we shut it off then there is baggage. Either way we need help to manage its hold on our lives. Keep your friends close to you and your enemies will be dismissed. No one can say they own you when you do not let them.

✓

"For some of us we may be glad such places exist. My computer suggested the title for this entry, the original title was singular. It conjures up certain images in our minds. They grey areas we do not want to admit exist in our psyche. In addition, we want our final resting place to be where there is no suffering. If it is anything like life then, I would say that; how I feel would depend on my attitude."

Mark 12:33 (KJV)

✓

Our Focus: None of us can reach for a reward we have not earned. Therefore, get right with yourself and you will be right with the Universe.

✓

"Many years from now we will feel different about what we experience today. Time can be an ally instead of, the enemy. Let us use our time wisely be mending the breaks in our lives that have gone awry. Do not leave the care of your loved ones to chance. Rekindle that original love you had for them and you will feel better about you."

Philippians 4:7 (KJV)

✓

Our Focus: Wherever your heart longs to be, ask yourself, why? Do you need to get uncomfortable to be comfortable? Finally, you must go to GOD to know what HIS will is because no one can tell you.

✓

"There is no virtue in getting everything you desire like the virtue in working for what you desire. Life will show up every day we are open to it. Change what needs to be changed whether you like It or not. Beat the odds at their own game. The ball is on your floor."

John 1:9 (KJV)

✓

Our Focus: There is more to satisfaction than keeping it. You are in position to share.
Are you going to be stingy?

✓

"We do not know what will happen tomorrow. All we can do is thinking of some way to manipulate outcomes. The unknown drives us all to the point of being afraid. The alternative is to get on your knees and ask for help. Put your thoughts in perspective by remembering who is in charge anyway."

1 Kings 4:29 (KJV)

✓

Our Focus: Knowing everything does not make us like GOD. We are but the channels of the Universe.

✓

"Some people want you to believe there is a right religion. Heaven and Hell are not real due to dogma. What happens to us upon death is a result of who we are not that we are dead. Experiences in life can bring great rewards yet, inexperience with life can be eternal costly."

Ecclesiastes 1:18 (KJV)

✓

Our Focus: Life does have some uncomfortable givens we must accept. One of the most important is that we do not get away with anything.

✓

"There were many times I scoffed at this word or concept. It did not make sense to me until; I believed that; to have it was the only thing that would keep me alive. Time was not my friend. There would come a time when I would have to give an account of my behavior. I have learned to pray and to pray for forgiveness. I know who I am not because I was told. I am confident that there is a Power greater than myself or anything that wants to judge myself."

Proverbs 16:16 (KJV)

✓

Our Focus: I have been redeemed.

"In my toughest class to date, I did my best work. I also got the most humiliated. My professor told me if it were about my test scores I would be nothing. However, reading this book you can see that: I write well. I have written for some of the best and they were impressed by my arrangement of words. The key was the simplicity of my sentences. Once, I mastered the punctuation I was in the know. Being such a student has groomed me to seek out how to serve. How may I help you? The challenge is putting my education to use through affecting change. I can and we can – Change the world."

Matthew 11:19 (KJV)

✓

Our Focus: You have more of an impact on someone's life than you know. Show up!!! COOL

Introspection: Week 12

Know that you have gifts. No one is born to get rich. Some of us are better at practice than others. Try to help someone before you help yourself. To me that is where the secret lies – in the way you treat the opportunities that come your way every day.

✓

"There are some situations as stressful as being a witness but, none as controversial. Did you know some religions require you to witness. However, you do not do it by freewill. There has to be an inspiration or a fundamental change in your psyche that moves you. I have never felt anything like it nor, has it repeated. Thank you LORD."

Psalm 49:3 (KJV)

✓

Our Focus: My mind and body collide on occasion. It produces some of my best intentions. Try to be in position to receive your blessing. Do not let it slip away.

✓

"Spirituality is not something you join. In fact, it is a personal journey many people take alone. My journey has permitted me limited contact with others outside of my duties. However, those who are in Light like me, still shape my way of communicating. We can share Light without exchanging Light. No need for instructions."

Psalm 119:104 (KJV)

✓

Our Focus: Make the day count when you count the days.

✓

"Sometimes it takes a great tragedy to unite a people. We have seen horrific events that ushered in this millennium. The "Willing Power" is the same whether written large or small. Take your rightful place – family is everything. GOD will not force HIS love on us for we must seek to receive."

Philippians 4:7 (KJV)

✓

Our Focus: Today, we have made a lasting bond with the Creator. Let us make our lives an example in compassion for the next generation. We should leave it better than we found it.

✓

"People label others based upon hearsay most of the time. For instance a neighbor may call you unclean as a response to her children talking about your home. We must not let our relationship with them fail. Stand for something so that you do not fall for anything. Then, you will be able to keep your friend while, you can correct the children. You could come out smelling like a rose."

Psalm 138:6 (KJV)

✓

Our Focus: We cannot save our face at the same time save our ass. We must choose what we believe. Disbelief can be very costly to others, not just ourselves.

✓

"As long as we can blame others there is no need to fear being accountable. You will start to feel better when you admit your mistakes. When you can see it is not about winning but how you played the game, then, you can claim success. Get out there and give it your best and when that does not work, do it better. A real motivation is knowing that there are people pulling for you to be victorious. If you are doing your best no one will be let down."

1 Corinthians 3:8 (KJV)

✓

Our Focus: To the best competitions we give all our attention. Winning is not the result of good spectating. Prepare, prepare, and prepare. That is what helps anybody to win.

✓

"I wish that I knew more about health and how it affects my daily life. I am lazy when it comes to making healthy changes yet; I seem to get lucky. I am now tobacco free and my life has changed overnight. Surrendering has been the most influential act that I have experienced this year. It helped me to graduate and to become more health conscious. I am aware of the benefits of managing my health with my doctor. I eat, pray, love, and meditate on a regular basis. These upgrades are producing a stronger more positive version of me. Listen to your voices."

1 Timothy 5:18 (KKJV)

✓

Our Focus: Let your conscience guide you're decision-making. There is plenty of help available. You are not alone anymore.

✓

"I have made great claims here. However, I will not make claims for you. Your life is not my responsibility. I only hope to, if you allow me, a chance to share some insights you may already have yet, you let them slip away. You will see that you can trust your thinking some of the time. I am only here to be of service."

Genesis 18:25 (KJV)

✓

Our Focus: I believe what we all want most is to feel comfortable with who we are.

✓

"I have seen many people act like they care. The ones that truly do will show up unannounced. Be good to yourself every day. It will be easier to think of others more than of yourself. When the "Willing Power can detect compassion in you It can then be more caring of your being when you need it. There are many ways to keep the HOPE alive in your life and the lives of those you care for."

Matthew 26:28 (KJV)

✓

Our Focus: Make time to break bread with loved ones. It truly is the best diet plan we all can do.

✓

"I have been successful in my rehabilitation as a direct result of community integration. Offering to be of service; paved the way for my tenure as a resident; in my town. My life has changed thus, I feel safe. The blessing is that those around me do not feel threatened."

Psalm 19:11 (KJV)

✓

Our Focus: Once we become more aware of the effect we have on others, we can act more responsibly and with greater care.

✓

"I try to treat others good and show respect. It seem as though my human condition presents obstacles to my empathy. I have been told that the solution is to face them head on. Then, I realized that; I made them myself. O, what a relief."

2 Timothy 4:14 (KJV)

✓

Our Focus: I know that I will never be perfect. I can live with that because, I have a GOD who is perfect and beyond perfect.

Introspection: Week 13

Remember, there are those who do not play fair. Also, being liked is not as important as being honest.

✓

"I count myself fortunate to have had two parents. My mother and father gave their all to raise a family. I was given many opportunities to achieve my goals. I had a lot of ambition. At time all I could say to my father was. I don't know." He did not like that he said it was a bad example for my brother. I thought I was being honest. Now, I know it was a form of contempt for my father. I am grateful my brother followed his heart."

Matthew 5:24 (KJV)

✓

Our Focus: Today, I know that I still influence my brother. Though he is younger, he displays great wisdom. I am proud to be his big brother.

✓

"I want to be the "right size" for my family. I could not survive without them. We have many fond memories of things we did that seem so important back then. Life was about secrets and toys. There was enough dirt to go around about everyone including yours truly. We have come such a far way since then. I am the age my parents were when they first tried to curfew me. Unfortunately, we were not raised in a democracy."

Galatians 6:7 (KJV)

✓

Our Focus: My dreams are becoming a reality. My conscience was void, not my heart. It is a gift to see the torch pass from generation to generation. There are changes and similarities. It is all the gift of life.

✓

"I have seen many memorable reunions. However, I do not remember some of my own Instead of jarring my memory, I recite a simple prayer to help and it keeps me calm. The "Willing Power" has it all in control. I need not be afraid and neither should you."

Psalm 147:5 (KJV)

✓

Our Focus: Some days there is nothing going our way. When such calamity strikes we would do well to keep our heads up and arms open. Someone may need a hug. NICE

"Sometimes I am unable to forgive anybody. I am stagnated by the fantasy of my ignorance. I want revenge. Subsequently, that handicap is being replaced by a more harmonious image and attitude. My satisfaction will be proportionate to my level of surrender. I know that being vindictive leads to family fallout. The, hurt people hurt people. It would be more gratifying to offer the same forgiveness I would want."

Philippians 4:7 (KJV)

Our Focus: Your life is in balance when those whom you love may come and go freely. No worries mate.

✓

"St. John 6:32 says, "… Moses gave you not that bread from heaven; but my Father giveth you the true bread from heaven." No servant can surpass his master therefore, give the LORD HIS due and you will be considered wise amongst your fellows."

John 6:32 (KJV)

✓

Our Focus: I am part of a group as a student. The group makes possible what individually is impossible. There is strength in unity. Join the group.

✓

"I have made a career out of doing things my way. Now, I count it foolish to isolate myself from others I did not realize this on my own. It is a wise idea to get help when you are in need of it. Arrogance can kill you."

Psalm 19:9 (KJV)

✓

Our Focus: Life is not meant to do alone. Let your heart soar, here is joy for you to find.

✓

"I am an uncle. I cannot imagine anything more joyful than the love of my nieces and nephew. GOFD has given me the privilege of seeing them become young women that take care of their son and nephew. We are not a perfect family but, family is the source of what is perfect."

Job 12:13 (KJV)

✓

Our Focus: My life is only passing like a plane flying overhead. I will try to keep the noise down.

Introspection: Week 14

My vision of life has changed over the years. I use to believe that I would be given everything I wanted. Reality was bitterly painful. Time does heal and permit healing. Growing up is a good thing.

✓

"I have become a morning person as I have matured. Actually, my parents reared me to be flexible when it involves supporting me. There are pros and cons for all types of situations we find ourselves in. Today, though; I am making better and healthier decisions. I have choices in my life that I could not tap into before. Changing my attitude has made some breakthroughs possible."

John 7:28 (KJV)

✓

Our Focus: I am humbled by the sacrifices my father and mother endured hard times to raise a family. They saw obstacles and they overcame them. That is the legacy they have passed on.

✓

"The best way for me to make that conscious contact with the Universe is through prayer. I am most alive when I share my heart with my Maker. The ties that I have established through daily prayer are strengthen when I rely on my GOD to provide me with what I need. Prayer is the new way I cover my tracks."

Romans 15:27 (KJV)

✓

Our Focus: I am the author of my own happiness. However, when things work out contrary to my expectations, I know that my editor has made other plans.

COOL

✓

"I always want to be in control. My life becomes shallow and insignificant when I try to manipulate situations. I am still trying to create the perfect balance of "sweet and sour" everything. I know where my strength originates. That Power has shown the utmost tolerance for me. I am amazed at the sheer grace that I receive on a continuous basis. It comes without ceasing. I must find the humility to share my good fortune."

Proverbs 18:10 (KJV)

✓

Our Focus: My world came crashing down around me about twenty three years ago. There was nothing that anyone could do to change what was happening except me. It had nothing to do with control.

April 18 _____ I don't want to wait in vain…

✓

"I have been on the edge days at a time. Here and now my enthusiasm has made me strong. I am not waiting in vain for love. No, I am giving the love I want to others because I feel loveable. Today, life needs more people who can bring something to the table other than their needs. My experience allows me to take a stand for what I believe in without shame or guilt."

Romans 1:11 (KJV)

✓

Our Focus: I have made many friends, (comma here not after but) but more acquaintances. I do not worry about who will last and who will leave. I just treat them as I want them to treat each other. The lasting relationships take work not reciprocity.

✓

"Many people feel there is a communication gap between parents and children. To bridge this gap, we have increased awareness and initiated some projects to help us all connect. Now, the time has come for those who know better to do better. Cherish your family for life would be less interesting without them. Not everybody gets two families."

Ephesians 5:8 (KJV)

✓

Our Focus: We must do our best to help the next generation feel safe in this country. Don't arm yourself, alarm yourself.

✓

"There are many ways to improve your circumstances. I was taught that charity begins at home. Therefore, you and I can choose to agree or to agree to choose what is best for each of us. I know for me the solution is waiting at home. Have a safe trip. Our paths may cross again when they do I will come ready to invite you to come with me."

Mark 1:4 (KJV)

✓

Our Focus: I have made many decisions in my life. One of my better ones was to remember where I came from. Thank you, mom and dad, for it all.

Does pride come before the fall?   April 21

✓

"There are days that I literary go hungry. I have no food or money. What do I do? I pray to the "Willing Power" for guidance and patience. Then in a few days I am able to eat again. Pride once ruled my life. Now, the grace and mercy of my Maker covers me. It is capable of taking care of me no matter what the challenge."

Psalm 49:6 (KJV)

✓

Our focus: The answers will come when we are in position, or condition, or intuition, to receive them. Consequences do not happen by accident.

Introspection: Week 15

Make the most of your higher consciousness. Remember, there is no decision based solely on what you want. The best part about service is that you do not have to search too far for someone in need.

✓

"I have learned to appreciate what is given to me. I try to live by my beliefs daily. That was not possible before I learned how to think about others. Heaven would be Hell if I were home alone and waiting. When you have the capability to help someone don't turn a deaf ear or a cold shoulder. It is worse than committing suicide."

Matthew 5:12 (KJV)

✓

Our focus: The "Willing Power" or GOD can render problems to nil. Therefore, I put my trust in HIM. Make your choice wisely because man cannot tell you more than he has experienced.

✓

"What if I were told that in four months I would lose my sight? I might rather be dead. I cannot prevent everything. In addition, I do not know the right thing to do. I don't want to go blind. If I accept it can I keep my vision? It does not work that way but, accept it anyway. After all, the doctor never has the final word."

Psalm 51:10 (KJV)

✓

Our Focus: My world is governed by a belief in humility and honesty. I cannot please everybody and myself all the time. There are no numbers. Then it…, it is better to work together.

✓

"We have some odd notions of good luck. Yet, I attribute never breaking a leg to having good luck and being blessed. I have never been told break a leg. Call me superstitious but, I did well in my math classes. Break a leg."

Luke 1:77 (KJV)

✓

Our Focus: My needs are different from my wants. The opposite fits as well. Good parenting has helped me to know the difference. Stop spoiling the children. Show them how to earn what they want and they shall have what they need.

✓

"It seems like learning has been given a bad rap. We get involved in activities that are dangerous. Yet, we have to read manuals, browse catalogues, and diagrams to do these activities. We need to come to the table and admit that we are missing something. The world is full of inexperience stuntman."

Galatians 6:7 (KJV)

✓

Our Focus: our current commander-in-chief is the first one in my memory to publicly admit a mistake while still in office. Wonderful!!!

✓

"I like to rush when I am doing something or anything I do not like. I despise going to Laundromats but, every week I am doing colors and whites. There is virtue in being your own man that is worth mentioning. Be patient the solution is on the way. It may not be what you think but, it will be what you need."

Mark 14:38 (KJV)

✓

Our Focus: All my chores have to be done. Now I go down waving the white flag. It has been a long time since I had it easy.

✓

"There are some things written in stone. However, life also gives us alternatives. Being willing to act on one could make the difference between life and death. It is no joke when you are forced to do something by force. You have to be connected to get the answer."

Titus 3:1 (KJV)

✓

Our Focus: In all my work I am capable of doing whatever is my best. I am making the decisions, yet there is still help out there.

✓

"I have been rehabilitated in part due to what I call "human conservation." People saw something meaningful in me. I do not know what but; I believe it was there. I sit here and now a supporter of recycling and preservation. To all who gave me the benefit of the doubt thanks?"

2 Corinthians 5:20 (KJV)

✓

Our Focus: I try very hard to not waste anything. It gets downright obsessive. However, I realize the implications of my efforts. Waste not want not is my new creed.

Introspection: Week 16

I keep my feelings private, there is great passion for what I believe in. I get my money's worth and I give my money's worth. Go green. It is good to be clean.

✓

"When my father lay helpless as a result from cancer, my love for him was unimportant. My duty as his eldest son was to make him comfortable. He told me he loved me then, he died." Taking care of him was a privilege I could not have earned but, was called to by my GOD and his."

Ecclesiastes 3:17 (KJV)

✓

Our Focus: Some things make all the difference in the world. My niche is being a relative – not many people can say that.

✓

"I am blessed beyond measure. My friends care about me without reservation. I am not alone in life anymore. I can talk about anything with my friends. When I lost my father, they made me strong. I could not have chosen better friends than the ones I received."

Matthew 5:24 (KJV)

✓

Our Focus: Remember, we were born into a family. There was no guarantee we would receive soul mates. Amazing!!!

✓

"I have friends that truly want the best for me. I feel the same way towards them. In fact, they are what is best for me. There is not much more pleasant a bond than the one that is shared with good friends. It took me most of my life to learn about friendship, but I would not have wanted to miss out on this gift."

Proverbs 4:5 (KJV)

✓

Our Focus: Some of our best relationships give us more than we give to it. Do not try to beat GOD when it comes to giving.

✓

"It seemed that as I grew older fear was not funny anymore. I would go to great lengths to avoid things I was afraid of. I use to go see horror films on my own. I had no idea how sheltered I was by what my parents did for me. Their love and devotion made life good for me that; I was not disturbed by too much. Some things we can learn without hitting our head against the wall. I am grateful for the life I have been given. Fear became stronger as time began to show me the truth about life. I still have not figured that one out."

Job 28:28 (KJV)

✓

Our Focus: I have been given much to appreciate in life. Could my fears be a reaction to the truth? It took me a long time to start saying thank you to my mother and father.

✓

"When I was younger my attention was stuck in what was said to me. My cousin calls me a late bloomer. At first she thought I was retarded. However, even I knew what retarded people looked like consequently, I thought she may have been a little slow. I learned to listen for better words then all those self-defeating labels. Her hold on my self-esteem began to disappear."

Proverbs 16:16 (KJV)

✓

Our Focus: My life is an array of people, places, and purposes that render me open to the will of GOD. I long to be of use to fulfill the promise of my forefathers.

✓

"Proverbs 3:7 says, "Be not wise in thine own eyes: fear the LORD, and depart from evil." The very notion of how to bring obedience into my life comes from the source of all that gives life meaning. The capacity to return to my childlike faith has proven to be the reinforcement to my new way of living,"

Proverbs 3:7 (KJV)

✓

Our Focus: I make my life flow when I step out of the control posture. Then, I submit myself to my LORD as I understand HIM.

✓

"I do the best I can to respect my nieces opinions about certain things they manage to get involved in. They are young women now and are becoming more independent each passing day. Despite my mistakes, they still care about me and honor my place in their lives. I know today that; I can be an example of family principles and values."

Daniel 12:3 (KJV)

✓

Our Focus: Sometimes the tears just flow when I reminisce about my rehabilitation. I used to curse the day I was born. Now, every day is like my birthday. I celebrate these birthdays by giving thanks to my family and GOD.

✓

"I use to think the "pursuit of happiness" meant to make as much money in the shortest amount of time that I could. What has change? The Chase is the same but; I am running a new race. I do not have to make a fortune anymore as I reclaim my life. Instead of a material motive, I have been taken in by the desire to serve my Creator. Get in shape to restore what was lost."

Proverbs 4:5 (KJV)

✓

Our Focus: I am learning how to live in my renewed sense of family and community.

✓

"Men have demonstrated with brutal competency his inclination to destroy what he has built. He has sacrificed much in the name of peace yet; there is still bloodshed in many of the developed nations of the world. We give weapons to the same people that are fighting those who are our allies. There must be something put between the creation and expiration of his own ability to run on his will."

Philippians 4: 8 (KJV)

✓

Our Focus: There can be peace in a world at war. When you leave your home today pray that you will return to it.

Introspection: Week 17

My friends, be not contemptuous beyond reason. There is much good that transpires every day. We just do not hear about it because we need to get involved. Allow the will of something greater than yourself to guide you. You will be impressed by the change that takes place.

"I have been able to favorably remember my first girlfriend crush. I was full of feelings but; I had no words. I felt like everything was a tongue twister. It was my lack of confidence that lessened my chances. This was the time in life where you either sink or swim socially. I was drowning in more ways than one. All I could hope for is that someday I would recover. The years have pottered my way with women. The secret is that they are people just like us men. It is okay that the one was the one that got away."

Colossians 1:9 (KJV)

Our Focus: Be grateful for our first loves. What I know now is that they are often the ones to teach us hard lessons to learn. We must learn them in order to pave the way for true love.

✓

"We have been playing games since our youth. The desire for distraction seems to grow with age. My favorite game is hide n' seek. I could be anyone I wanted. It was fun to be a different person but; in real life we cannot control who we are only ourselves. Life was meant for us to stay in character as much as we could. For our blessings come with our name on them. No one is meant to receive what is for me."

Revelation 19:11 (KJV)

✓

Our Focus: My faith allowed me to pay without fear. I know that HE cares for me today as well.

✓

"I have received my courage from my LORD. Today, I can be with HIM and not feel ashamed. The obedience starts in my thinking for the change is coming. HE does not encumber me with the shortcomings of my past. My LORD gives me rest from my labors while. I am leaning on HIS name for my hope. HE is the strength in my weaknesses and my faults. There is none like HIM in my world."

Job 12:13 (KJV)

✓

Our Focus: Courage is not the lack of fear, but the presence of grace and mercy when you are afraid. When GOD reveals his wondrous ways there is no need to fear.

✓

"The first time I heard this, I went to the bathroom and gazed into the mirror. I was very young with an ego that could fill the pages of this book. I just knew that I had the looks in my family for that was what made me feel good about me. I became the envy of my family making sure everything was color coordinated. However, nothing was ever good enough. There was something that always needed fixing.'

John 1:9 (KJV)

✓

Our Focus: Make time for yourself to relax. Do not keep on pushing the envelope. The grass is sometimes greener on the side your standing. Take time to smell the roses.

✓

"Respect your parents by passing along the lessons they taught you to your children. Both my parents were great teachers. They had their issues but; I learned how to listen to mom and dad. At times they told me some personal stuff about themselves giving me a real inside look into my history. I learned a lot about myself from our talks that made me feel privilege to be the older son. They were on the same page most of the time. That is what made them so appealing to my attention"

1 Peter 1:18 (KJV)

✓

Our Focus: I learned how to focus from listening to my father. I loved the attention and I imagine he did also.

I am broke!!!   May 13

✓

"I lived many years being afraid I would not have enough money to support myself. Now, there is faith and hope where there was doubt. There are things I can do to help myself. I do not have to live off of soup kitchens for the rest of my life. I have seen that they do not make anything better. I do not like eating when I cannot choose what I want. My needs are the priority in my life. Sometimes I do not have a choice still but; I don't stand in a line anymore for what someone wants to give me. What a miracle."

Exodus 15:2 (KJV)

✓

Our Focus: Many thanks to all my friends for their words of wisdom and those care packages. Thank you for everything. It was really kind of you.

✓

"I have learned that sometimes the smartest thing I can do is ask the question. Is is a great relief to surrender that know-it-all attitude. I could barely stand it myself. That is a very lonely place to be when you think that you hold the keys to everyone's dilemma. My family and I are very happy about my new attitude."

Ecclesiastes 9:16 (KJV)

✓

Our Focus: I hope that when my eyes go dim(comma and delete "that) that, I will not be running low on life. I just want to fade away like a robust spring into the sunny bright days of summer.

Introspection: Week 18

My opinion counts just as much as the next person. I just do not always make it public anymore. Some things are better left unsaid. When I talk I do not want to just hear myself. Learning how to keep my mouth closed has brought many great gifts.

✓

"We all can place this high on the priority list. It is a principle we take for granted. It is much easier we sometimes think to lie. Paradoxically, I too have struggled with honesty. There were times I could swear that the truth was just too painful to say. Or, I thought that I would get beat if I told the truth. So, I am no authority on the matter of truth or dare. I have endured much turmoil trying to play GOD. This is an area I have not surrendered to my Higher Power yet; I have an abundance of experience that all will be okay. I ask only that you blaze your own path I can see the light at the end of the road and I am not in a tunnel."

James 1:19 (KJV)

✓

Our Focus: It was an attribute that I took for a joke. I will continue to practice honesty in mu (typo) speaking and my behaving. I have gotten much better

✓

"There is nothing more repulsive than violence. To our men and women in uniform we share a heartfelt gratitude for your sacrifice and your willingness. As I have seen it, the willingness for your duty as soldiers and guardians of the free is the key factor is your honorable service. I believe that should war have been pleasant that, you still would have served. May GOD keep you and your loved ones close to grace with HIS love. Do not rain on your own parade. Help us to be better and more conscious of what you were asked to do by GOD almighty, keep up the good work. Violence ought to be left to the experts not to us laypeople."

Luke 3:14 (KJV)

✓

Our Focus: Violence is a multi-billion dollar business. Abstain from violence to avoid being a victim of it. We all a survivor of violence in the world today. Honor their blessing by alternative methods of self-expression. Be a part of the solution not the problem.

✓

"I have no friends or relatives that are police or serving in the Armed Forces. Our liberties and freedom are priceless to each individual in uniform. There are tragedies that arise from bed judgment calls. The survivors are often left with no answers to comfort them. It is the work of the LORD that will make the hurt these people feel subside. The challenge we face is the bitterness associated with such a senseless act. I have been an eyewitness to such intimidation as well as, a survivor. I can tell you that my friend and I were in the wrong. We brought the attention to ourselves."

Psalm 49:3 (KJV)

✓

Our Focus: I am forever grateful to those who serve. They have thought long and hard about that sacrifice.

✓

"I always thought that people trusted me. I was right to a certain extent. For the care of my life, I put my trust in my parents. Later, it became my brother whom is younger than me. My brother guided me towards a relationship with my GOD of my understanding. GOD is my power greater than myself, my Higher Power, and my "Willing Power." HE is all in one go to guy." If it were about cards HE would be the gambit. GOD earned my attention and I mean my full attention."

John 1:9 (KJV)

✓

Our Focus: People are in need of guidance in this new Millennium. Be considerate by pointing them in the right direction.

✓

"This is an issue for some of us to humbly face head on. It can be uncomfortable while being critically unrewarding. From my experience there is little control I have over the situation at hand. In addition, it is not always necessary. Some things are meant to keep to yourself. Today, I know that and I made the right call. My focus is not on looking good to the other half at all. I want to be forgiven by GOD for my sins in this life."

John 15:1 (KJV)

Our Focus: When it is time for introspecting your life, take it day by day. Examine the most pressing issues first. You will make the time to change.

✓

"Growing up I was taught to listen to adults in order to be liked by them. It was hard when they asked me questions. Most of the time I responded with, "I don't know." That was my answer for everything. I did not believe I could answer questions for them about anything including myself. I thought I was being honest but; it got old quick. What saved me were my manners. I knew how to say please and thank you and may I!! It was a very stressful time in my life for. I had my friends that looked up to me. They trusted me to tell them the truth without any improvising. The fun was fading from my life yet; I was adapting well-thank you grandma."

Proverbs 3:5 (KJV)

✓

Our Focus: Do not make enemies when you can make friends. Good manners are key to survival.

✓

"It is amazing how we are able to support ourselves and the ones we love every day. We are vessels of a benevolent power rich in resources that supplies our needs. Therefore, be generous when you can without delay. There is only a world of gratitude and compassion waiting for you as you look for your service niche. The quality of your service efforts will show to those at your side. May you continue to develop the skills and insight for your work as the LORD allows. Make today count."

Acts 9:15 (KJV)

✓

Our Focus: Nowadays, the woman is also a provider; she can be acknowledged for it today. There is no more hiding in the shadows. The blessing of a nation depends on its opportunities available to its women. They bring life into this world perhaps, such a responsibility will be recognized and respected.

Introspection: Week 19

I can make a blunder of my daily life when I go without my "fides qua creditur" or act of faith. It is not just talking and listening to GOD but, acting in HIS likeness for the glory of HIS kingdom. My place in HIS world will be the result of the belief I have in HIS word. I know that all those whom have spoken life into my life were acting on the will of my Creator. We are waiting for you...

✓

"Death can be very painful for all involved. Only in America could there be superstitions around something this intimate. I was with my father as he crossed over from certainty to eternity. I hoped that I helped him by telling him I loved him. There was still some unfinished business between us yet; we have to carry on. MY dad is still a presence in my life. Someday I know that I will receive a revelation about my father that will make everything alright."

"Many of us shudder with memories of loved ones we lost. If there were any words I could say to ease your pain I would. Some days it just helps to be there with you or even here. May you joyfully recall all the precious moments of your life with them."

Mark 12:33 (KJV)

✓

Our Focus: Life is never easy and death does not give us any reassurance. I realized that the LORD thought of me too. To GOD be the glory and majesty.

✓

"Today, I want to poke at your heart to make you aware of how much you mean to me. Whenever I need a shoulder or an ear, there you are. Thank you for your compassion and concern. I cherish our heart to heart-my child. May the LORD shine HIS light of mercy and favor on you? You have made my days fresh in the daylight and sweet in the evening."

Psalm 31:12 (KJV)

✓

Our Focus: When we humble ourselves the help is always available. Remember, GOD deal(s) in eternity, not the temporal cues of the day. HE is infinite. We are finite.

✓

"She was the lift in my spirit, she was the "multiple in my joys", and she is the quiet before my storms. I miss her without ceasing. In addition, I was blessed to be her boy while loving her as her son. No one will ever take your place-MOM. I will forever love you mother my queen. May GOD shine HIS light of grace and mercy on me for any of my failings to you?"

2 Corinthians 4:7 (KJV)

✓

Our Focus: My life has been blessed beyond measure. All that I am due I will receive. For I know that no man can cancel GOD"S plans.

✓

"In a particular faith, people are taught to love their enemies and to pray for those that use them. That is an odd request, no? Well, I thought it would be easy for my enemies would want to be in my shoes were they inclined to this religion. I could do it until my heart took over. I worked diligently at it and I still became wroth. May GOD have mercy on me? The day will come when I am in need of such a type of forgiveness as this."

Ecclesiastes 9:11 (KJV)

✓

Our Focus: Ask for forgiveness for it is better to give than to receive in matters of the heart.

✓

"When I learned about faith, I was in need of redemption. Later, I discovered man could not give me such a gift as absolution. The only body that can do that is the blood and body of CHRIST. There are things that have happened which, go beyond rational dissemination. I was witnessed to them to be able to claim the LORD as my savior and my LORD. I do not doubt that for a minute. The things the LORD did were not the type of happenings that came up in table talk or pillow talk. However, they were enriching to the soul."

"It is the power of HIS word that saved my faith. I had all but given up on miracles when I wanted to take my own life. Then who would fulfill my needs? Be true to your faith and there HE will meet you. GOD does anything but fail."

1 Corinthians 15:44 (KJV)

✓

Our Focus: I am a power of example for my nieces today. I have no greater gift than the respect of my family and friends.

✓

"Many times I have wanted to hear the right words. I started to recite them in prayer. The greatest love is the love for friends. MY words have great meaning to them. It is my life purpose to see my friend s happy and home. I am at a loss for words many times that I am called on to give advice. However, the only thing that comes from my mouth is what they need to heat but, not what I thought I could say."

Psalm 3:8 (KJV)

✓

Our Focus: Treat others like you want to be treated. Then, your words will matter as well as your actions. Talk is cheap I heard; however it is plentiful.

✓

"I have been released from the bondage of self. NO longer do I need to act against my nature. Experience has taught me how to be empathetic. It is a lot less stressful than planning my revenge. Thinking of others like I think of myself has softened my heart. I have stopped taking others' kindness for weakness. I understand what giving is about and why we all should do it. I like to give when I am in need it seems to show me who is really watching over this place. HIS way are unlike our ways."

Philippians 2:12 (KJV)

✓

Our Focus: When we try something without judging it first we increase our level of satisfaction. Let others in on the secret.

Introspection: Week 20

Make your life easier. Surrender to your selfishness, then try to be more generous. After you admit your selfish ways you can regain control. You are no longer a victim. Do not let the past dictate how you will live today. You can correct almost anything that is haunting you. Give it your best.

✓

"Gratitude is an action not just a feeling. It goes better for us when we include in our grand scheme a way to demonstrate our gratitude. It is best shown when we choose to live with some accountability for our actions. We do not just live as thought our opinions matter more than the next person's. Gratitude shows in how we live. Intrinsically, we know when we are taking things for granted. And when we have great respect for the kindness we receive. My parents always did their best to make sure I knew that I was fortunate to be where I was."

"The new attitude in my life has a lot to do with gratitude. I have been on the receiving end of gratitude for something I did for someone many years ago. I helped someone get off narcotics and pick up their lives. They tell me it was the best gamble they ever took. They said that they could finally believe in themselves because e, somebody believed in them. That was the nicest compliment I ever received."

Isaiah 12:2 (KJV)

✓

Our Focus: We show our gratitude by the way we relate to the world around us. Don't keep it all to yourself. It is real cool to share it. Watch it grow.

✓

"It is superstitious or for a select few to not believe in luck. I thought that it was always against me. I use to go fishing with some friends and I would be the only one not catching fish. I could catch the bottom feeders that nobody wanted. The trophy fish; I could not even get a bite. I was not going to take the credit for their good luck. I wanted some of my own. I thought that GOD hated me. The angels were laughing at me and I felt stupid. I did not believe in luck because, I had no reason to believe in luck. It really made me feel like GOD did not like me. I never got over it."

Titus 2:11 (KJV)

✓

Our Focus: I do not leave much to chance. That is being irresponsible, right?

✓

"Some people think they are wise when they tell you. "If you want to make GOD laugh make plans." I did not hear HIM laugh on 9-11-01. There was nothing funny on that day. Forgive me, LORD."

Isaiah 61:10 (KJV)

✓

Our Focus: We can make our lives better when we help others to do the same. It is better to give a lesson than to limit our blessings.

✓

"Professionals had to practice their talents in repetition to become experts. The most difficult part in learning is learning the difficult part. To become proficient at prayer requires a commitment like that you have for learning. We get better at those things we do again and again. It is a simple equation for complicated people like us. If you want something in this life you have to work at it."

Luke 6:12 (KJV)

✓

Our Focus: We are making progress now the next step is to continue to make the effort. You may not be perfect at first, but down the road you will have the answers.

✓

"It has been said that you can never get enough money. Some days I feel like I missed the boat. I knew money was not easy to get growing up yet; there is a lot of opinions about money. People feel the rich get richer while; the rest of us fight for what is left. Contrary to popular myth, money can make you happy but; it will not keep you that way. The money will be used daily as we try to cling to our past. I see myself as money mature. Do your best to keep money in its place."

1 Timothy 6:10 (KJV)

✓

Our Focus: Do not make getting rich your sole priority. Money does not buy everything. The most important gift you can receive is priceless. It is not sold in stores or online. All that is required is that you meet the right person.

✓

"I have been witness to the effects of gravity on the human body. There are pros and cons to the way our vanity; is subject to the distortion, gravity does to us daily. I like to have my feet on the ground like they always have been. However, a tummy tuck might be nice. Procedures were never my favorite past time. Be careful about what you choose to do with your image. The effects last forever."

Acts 8:20 (KJV)

✓

Our focus: Being humble makes life more fun. Now, you can loosen up. Relax, it only gets better from here. You've had your last fix.

✓

"I know that he made many sacrifices to take care of me while, he single-handedly gave or his time, money, and health. There was nothing too good or bad that I wanted. He never left me when I was broke. He picked me up without knowing how to. You are a hero-DAD."

Micah 6:8 (KJV)

✓

Our Focus: He was many things to a lot of good people. Happy Birthday- "Poppy."

✓

"If it has ever happened to you then, there is a time to want revenge. However, the "Willing Power" can grant us the capacity for forgiveness. Believe that there will come a day when we stand in need of that very same forgiveness. What you put into your faith you get out of it. Faith is an intangible part of us we can apply to our lives but; do not let yours be grounded in wanting something for nothing. Be willing to give what you want and life will seem almost fair."

Psalm 103:8 (KJV)

✓

Our Focus: Let bygones be bygones. Really!!!

✓

"I have had the task of risking my life for someone I love. At the time it was hard to choose. The thought that impacted my decision most was who would care. I could not be torn any more than what I was that day. I will not tell you my answer for something's are meant to keep to yourself. We are both happy today still."

Matthew 6:25 (KJV)

✓

Our Focus: People do not believe the right thing will happen, they believe what happens may not be the right thing.

However we know we are not in control.

✓

St. John 1:4 says, "In HIM was life, and the life was the light of men." The wonderful birth of the Messiah was witnessed in a sign by many at the time. Those whom count themselves faithful know the significance of that continuity. The miracle was done for the salvation of all who would believe yet; He was treated no better than a common criminal. Do not let appearances dictate your next response to the situation. The solution has already been in effect. Now, you must get in position to receive what is for you."

John 1:4 (KJV)

Our Focus: Let your faith help you to stand when there is trouble. We want to repent when HE comes.

Introspection: Week 21

When I make my prayer to GOD, I can feel the release from my cares of this world. My goal is to share the truth with others and to make that truth a part of my life by the witness of others. I use to need people to tell me how good GOD has been to me. Today, I can acknowledge that myself.

✓

"I have experienced the miracle of hope. It can make what is old seem new, what is broke seem better, and what is bad seem good. Whatever the struggle is let hope be what makes the difference. You are better off with some hope than without any. It will save the day. For a long time I had no hope subsequently, there was no connection or awareness of a power that could help me have the type of life I wanted. In addition, the people I saw living a life like I wanted did not all have hope. Some of them were simply very industrious. Those that did show hope told me they would not want it any other way. Miracles do happen to us all."

Hebrews 6:19 (KJV)

✓

Our Focus: What we gain by hope, by hope we gain. Fulfill the promise.

✓

"We as prayer warriors need only to look inward for the answer. What is the Helper? For me the Helper is the sacrament of communion. I participate as a way of showing myself humbled by HIS word. As a child that is what I was told. I believe! There is a certain security that only GOD can give. I could not find it anywhere else. The journey of faith is meant to experience with others however, we try to make others believe like we do. That can be counterproductive. Allow others to have their belief in order, that the group is what grows stronger. The journey is personal. Do not try to make others like you believe they do not believe."

1 Peter 3:15 (KJV)

✓

Our Focus: We know that we fall short of the glory of GOD. We receive HIS grace when we believe. That is the promise not a contract.

✓

"I like to think that I am reliable. However, in my humanness the most I can claim is that; I can follow direction. I do not cause the sun to set, to shine, or the moon to rise. I rely on a power greater than myself. That belief has been the cornerstone of my life resurrection. I am able to keep the important things in their proper perspective for, my own power is enhanced by the power greater than myself. People count on me because, they know I will do what I need to in order to complete the job or favor."

Romans 5:4 (KJV)

✓

Our Focus: the rewards of life come by work, however, the rewards of heaven come by grace. Both come from that one authority whom shares with who HE wants.

✓

"My mind has not seen the opportunities of life before now. Whatever I decided to do can become reality. I thank my family for their encouragement. There was always the promise of a better life for that is the desired result of all the hard work they did. Paradoxically, the challenges to achieving that life are the attraction to a young person like I was. I was fortunate, the influence of my parents was stronger than the streets. I am forever in their hearts and mind. They will always be the glow in my shine."

Isaiah 57:215 (KJV)

✓

Our Focus: Choose whom you will serve but choose wisely.

✓

"We are called on in times of trouble to serve. However, there may also be some changes that have to be made. So, let your heart serve with gladness. He has got the whole world in the palm of HIS hand. There is no greater love than the love of GOD. It is unconditional in its origin and it is given freely."

Acts 20:19 (KJV)

✓

Our Focus: Together we can climb the highest mountain. If you want to live forever then pray with someone.

✓

"We do better in conversation when we think before we speak. I had to learn this skill the hard way. Now, I practice it regularly. I choose my words carefully for ignorance carries a heavy load. There is no better gift we have than the moment of silence where we can gather our thoughts and present tem in a constructive orderly fashion. Rambling was never attractive to me. I like knowing what I am saying."

Proverbs 12:18 (KJV)

✓

Our Focus: Before you venture into the social life, make some boundaries to protect yourself as well as others. Keep your eyes wide open at any cost.

✓

"For the care of all concerned, there are many little perks that help keep life as simple as it can be. These small miracles have their way of appearing right when we need them. Courage to explore life as a participant can bring catastrophic changes that really make a difference in how we live. This is all orchestrated by a divine presence which we call by many different titles. The important thing is to accept that we do have limitations as humans. Fire is hot and makes things hot."

Psalm 24:4 (KJV)

✓

Our Focus: I have made major changes in my life, opening new possibilities. I will get what is best for me.

Introspection: Week 22

Make no mistake, I do not cry wolf over a fox. To be distressed means that there will be some fallout. However, I will sleep in my bed after I make it. We are all accountable for the places we find ourselves in. The only victims are the ones we leave behind when we have been rash.

"The ability to feel fear was my adolescent goal. It was a goal because, at that time in my life we were taught to not show any fear. Now, when I am afraid it makes me nervous. I feel sometimes as if I were going backwards instead of forwards. It could be from too much fear. Doing things that were scary was how I proved my manhood. I still felt like me I could do things that others did not do. I felt like I was better than others. Today. I associate fear with violence which, makes it less attractive to be afraid."

Psalm 56:4 (KJV)

Our Focus: Life can be frightening at any time other than when it is planned. Moderation is the key to control your fear. Face it, break it, and replace it. It does get better.

✓

"We are fortunate enough to have learned other ways of resolving conflicts. The most important part is to deal with them in the moment. Today, there is no need to make the situation any worse. The more we practice a constructive was of resolution the easier it is to allow others to be themselves. In any conflict there will be different opinions yet; we all want the same thing. In such situations; there is a way to diffuse the moment with some carefully thought out decisions. Then, we can proceed confident that we have done our best."

Job 12:13 (KJV)

✓

Our Focus: There is a place for powerful people. The only power one needs in that place is awareness. Living skills do not come in handy when you are there.

✓

"There is a brighter day at hand. This year has been defined by some memorable events. There is one many people celebrated tonight. To the Captain, "My hope for you is to always be an influence for you were made by an influence." Congratulations! The kicker is that I like the neighbors – get it. (LOL) You are the tops."

Proverbs 24:5 (KJV)

✓

Our Focus: Respect is a commodity that would leave the market on the brink if trading were low. Keep investing there will be others in all shapes and sizes.

✓

"This is like a grudge match with an opponent who never shows up. How could anyone hold to such a belief when you have to believe? I say to hell with the concept of no pain-no gain. I cannot even fathom what that is like. If I were of that belief, I would have been dead long ago. All people need to aspire to do things that require them to sacrifice some deeply held opinions and preferences."

'In such circumstances as I have experienced, there was always the air of possibility. I knew that I was not alone nor could I think that I was able to impact any consequences had it not been for a power other than human. My convincing you does not help me because it is not supposed to. That is part of being of service. The work is done to glorify HIM.

Exodus 15:2 (KJV)

✓

Our Focus: We truly live in the "melting pot." There is room for everybody.

✓

"My father use to tell me I eat too fast. Food has always made me feel good. I share that blessing with others. Friends show up and I feed them. It is a blessing to enjoy your meals. I have gotten into eating more healthy foods. They are just as satisfying to me as my favorite candy bar. It does take some time to get use to but; healthy habits grow on you like the bad ones do. The choice is yours."

Ecclesiastes 9:11 (KJV)

✓

Our Focus: We must continue to raise awareness about the plight of those with eating disorders. We can stop their suffering in silence. We are their voice.

✓

"Sometimes we become burdened by a crutch. A crutch can help you stand but; can you stand the pain without the crutch? We have grown accustomed to a quick fix attitude. That type of thinking is futile for in time we will need to be able to bare pain. All pain is meant to give us information about ourselves perhaps; that is the fault of the pain. Historically, it takes a great circumstance to make us look at who we are. It should be a requirement for us all to be able to assess our lives with great compassion. There is much to learn from introspection."

Joel 3:10 (KJV)

✓

Our Focus: the problem did not start with us. However, we are in the best position to create change. Let the spirit of belonging be your motivation.

✓

"Today, I have the gift of hindsight. It helps me to stop making the same mistakes. My daily routine can change at any moment. I must not be motivated by the rigidity of certainty. I like when can roll with the punches. My life has been sent into turmoil before by no fault of mine own. I did have a part in the incident however, I was not treated like I was accustomed to. I learned that no one is perfect but; my reaction is more important than my position. If I can make my life a reflection of the many positions I find myself in then, I can make my life reflect the position I want to be in."

"I do concur that life is what we allow it to be. It seems that we have to say no to anything that feels good. That is not so when you have a belief system that works for you. It must be derived from your faith or it amount to naught. Take the bull by the horns and let your experience be the reference point of you future decisions."

Ephesians 1:3 (KJV)

✓

Our Focus: My wish for you is to always feel like each day is new. May your joys are multiplied.

Introspection: Week 23

There have been moments I have suffered. Yet, I know that no one can hurt me more than I. <u>H</u>elp <u>O</u>ne <u>P</u>erson <u>E</u>veryday – H.O.P.E. Today, I know that no one can hurt me more than myself.

✓

"When I think about my love interest, I kick myself because they all failed. There was intense attraction and chemistry. It was like buying a used car without a warranty. The sign said "as is" but still, it could be better. I will not pay a commission for misery again. The only thing I had going for me was my consistency with being present. I could not have been more disappointed than I was with romance. I am no longer inclined to think romance is meant to last forever. Pleasure is part time while discipline is for eternity."

Romans 1:11 (KJV)

✓

Our Focus: Let today be the start of taking things at face value. Do not read into every incident in your life from day to day. Suit up then show up.

✓

"As a child life seemed a lot simpler. I took many things for granted. I did not foresee any of the challenges I have faced. Everything a person needs I was given. There was no complaining. When the family secrets started to surface, life was disrupted. They can be detrimental to the family unity. My identity was in question yet; I did not feel any different. All I know is that these secrets seemed to be more important than the daily routines of our home. The only thing wanted was to keep what I had. Subsequently, that is just what I lost. Everything was taken from me by my own father which, made me question who he really was. It was the most horrible thing a parent could do. Now, I was going to need a friend that was better than my best friend."

1 Corinthians 10:3 (KJV)

✓

Our Focus: The secrets can tear a family apart because of the shame they carry. Embrace your loved ones and let that love be more important than our judgments.

✓

"Some things are over rated. Soul food is not one of them. You have to find the right place and order only what speaks to you. I know my best dish but; I do not have it very often. When you have these two requirements then, there will be time. The result will be an experience into the culture appeal of making your own dish."

Psalm 27:1 (KJV)

✓

Our Focus: I am blessed to have experienced some of the finer things in life. To whom much is given there is much required-the truth.

✓

"There are few stories more captivating than romances. It offers the delicacies in life for the taking. It does involve a degree of courage. You must tame the heart of another. All who engage are the hunters and the hunted? The sporting world is not all about violence. Proceed with great caution for now your heart is at stake."

Psalm 46:1 (KJV)

✓

Our Focus: When we give our heart there will be no safety net.

✓

"My Parents taught me right and wrong. They allowed me to make certain decisions. There were still rules I had to obey. They did not compromise the standard. The structure was put in place to help me and to keep me safe. I had the utmost respect for their efforts. My parents did all they could to make our home a safe place. To learn and play. We did not have to do much except for some simple chores that made it less hectic for them to do their chores. I thought that a family was the greatest gift one could have. I loved my family even with my shortcomings. There was no place like home."

Philippians 2:12 (KJV)

✓

Our Focus: Being successful starts early in life. A big part of it is how you treat others. Do not be fooled by what you see on television.

✓

"My faith is in the grace and mercy of GOD. I do not waiver from my relationship with HIM. For trials and temptations come every day. With HIS word I can rise above any difficulty."

Luke 19:9 (KJV)

✓

Our Focus: My life will be an example to those coming after me. By that, I am humbled.

✓

"Many times we have lost ourselves in very stimulating conversations. Let our talk be the impetus for change. The greatest aspect of this country is that –there is always work to do. Become a part of the solution than you will see that we are all fighting for the same things. There are many different ways to accomplish the same goal. Cultural awareness is not a bad thing. We will be motivated by many people in our lifetime. There are many contributors the common welfare of us all."

Psalm 3:8 (KJV)

✓

Our Focus: Make the day count. Then, you can claim it was a good day.

Introspection: Week 24

We will fall short trying to please everyone. The most we can do is improve by amending our attitude. If we are lucky change will take place. There is always hope for us because GOD set it up that way.

✓

"Life is shaped in part by who we listen to. The voices of reason keep the distortions to a minimum. When we live by the principles we were taught then, the voices of reason will protect us."

Titus 2:11 (KJV)

✓

Our Focus: Try to adhere to your schedule for it will be the discipline others will hear that they emulate. Stay the course without distraction. Consider 'for it will be that discipline that others may emulate. Stay….)

✓

"How do the needs of others count to us? When you think of someone as much as yourself then, you may be called a saint. We will put in overtime because, the Light shines our way. There is great blessings in being considerate of the needs of others. Do not get caught up the attitude of self-centeredness for there is no lonely road then to think it is all about you. Kindness is never weak like hope it expands."

Hosea 14:9 (KJV)

✓

Our Focus: Make your work a testimony to your gratitude. Anything else would miss the mark. Be in the process of success every day.

✓

'Growing up meant becoming like mom and dad. That seemed very difficult to me. I suspected that there was not much fun in the trade off. However, I also perceived that I would get respect. Mom and dad were not wrong. They gave me a valid example to follow. It took me awhile but; I got with the program."

1Peter 5:5 (KJV)

✓

Our Focus: Raise your children with a GOD conscious and they will not have to be alone. Nor will you.

✓

"This is a line from a spiritual I sang in church on many Sundays. It gave me a jolt when I pondered its meaning. I cannot fathom what HIS second coming will be like. However, there will be a place for everyone to see…"

Haggai 2:7 (KJV)

✓

Our Focus: To some degree we have all considered how we would be changed by HIM. Let us keep our expectations small and our gratitude large.

✓

"The dictionary defines *diligence* with clear, concise, and insightful language. We would be wise in learning how to practice this principle. Lives may be saved. Lives will be changed and then we can change the world. Just imagine the world without its worst condition, for example-AIDS then, we will begin to get a picture of how it was meant to be."

Isaiah 26:8 (KJV)

✓

Our Focus: Make the goal for today to extend some kindness where it is needed. It just may make your day as well as someone else's.

✓

"As a nation we share certain desires. One such desire is to feel safe here at home. Many men and women defend that desire at the cost of their lives. Let us make certain they do not fight in vain. Do your civic duty when it pertains to the welfare of our home. Keep sending your representatives to speak where we all need to have a voice. Let us not neglect to remember there was a time when some of this country's citizens had no voice or representation. That is a time that is better revisited than relived."

Psalm 145:16 (KJV)

✓

Our Focus: We are at a turning point in history. There will be no more tragedies for our sins when we can find the humility to repent of them. Don't wait to be shone someone else's way. Go with what is in your heart.

✓

"Imagine if we were to make major decisions solely on the basis of how we felt. Life would seem very unkind to many. I would be one of those in that group. Paradoxically, many decisions due involve our feelings, some of which are at a very personal level. We must make that connection from head to heart. Feelings are not the enemy but; they must be kept in the context of the situation at hand."

Psalm 51:6 (KJV)

✓

Our Focus: The mind is an ally when it comes to priorities. In such cases, using this discipline will assure you of things panning out. Stay the course.

✓

"There is a shift in what we are willing to tolerate. Those of us who know someone going through correction are supportive of their cause. The LORD corrected those HE loved therefore, we ought to accept the torch and carry it. When it comes down to the principles we all need to improve our attitudes."

Proverbs 3:11 (KJV)

✓

Our Focus: A firm show of unity is what made my parents' love last until they passed on. Together is how we were raised. I am thankful for their dedication.

✓

John 11:27 says, "…I believe that thou art the CHRIST, the son of GOD, which should come into the world." This woman could hear the LORD'S authority in HIS voice. Her faith needed no other proof. We need to build our faith through the efforts we give each day. The LORD is one of the most approachable people you will ever meet when you take the risk of letting Him in. End your loneliness by inviting JESUS into your life. HE will lift more than your spirits."

John 11:27 (KJV)

✓

Our Focus: we have much to learn about faith. Perhaps what we are really doing is relearning. Being cynical is no shortcut. It is a steep cliff.

Introspection: Week 25

We humans could not possibly be our own Creator. There is much about this life which still troubles us. The challenges today demand that we look inward at our self. Do you want to keep what you see? If not, look at it from HIS point of view. Try then change what has to be changed.

✓

"When we indulge in gossip or other forms of dishonesty, there is going to be differences of opinions. If what we want is confidence there is a shift required in our perspective. Let your principles guide your social life. The peculiar things that make u gossip are not going to cause you to miss out on anything that may be helpful."

Ephesians 2:10 (KJV)

✓

Our Focus: There are better ways to stay in touch with what is happening in your social world. Try to get out more with friends. You are probably isolating yourself for no good reason at all.

✓

"I have fond memories of church over the years I spent there. There I learned that I was not religious as these folks were. I was more inclined to spirituality. Religion is a life all its own. Today, I live more by my faith in contrast to religion. I would not call it going to church. The term I have learned is fellowship. I fellowship today with others who have their own ideas about faith. Mine have worked for me before I knew they would. Faith can grow on you like a promotion on a new job. I always knew I was to serve but; I did not know how to."

"Make no mistakes there is a job description to serve. You may be in an undesirable place yet; you know it is where are meant to serve. Can you just pick up and leave? I would dare say no. Your faith has delivered you to where you can do the most good. It is your duty to serve with gladness. Give HIM the praise so the blessings will come down."

2 Corinthians 5:17 (KJV)

Our Focus: Place your trust in the "Willing Power" for there is where you will find peace. It is a peace unknown to many.

✓

"On the day HE was crucified CHRIST gave HIS disciples' one last commandment. HIS "fides qua creditur"or act of faith was an impetus that later brought them together. They were witness to the greatest feat GOD had ever performed. HE told them to love one another as HE loved them. With respect to what they witnessed, there could have been no other thought than HIS last words. In all honesty I do not envy those men nor HIS mother for they saw the horror of the violence HE suffered. I only hope to be counted amongst the faithful at HIS return."

Luke 19:9 (KJV)

✓

Our Focus: The commandments are like the beginning of knowledge of GOD. This is to demonstrate HIS authority and our fear of or respect for HIS divinity. Proceed with great caution.

✓

"It was a lesson that proved to be a very useful method to attract girls. I wanted to be perfect yet, I did not know the right words to say. The girls had it easy because, all they had to do was smile. I had to "woo" them but, I had to figure out what "woo" meant. I had no clue. Then, I did it It was working for me and I did not even know it. I gave them a lesson- I scored. The girls were lining up for my lessons at all the parties. I thought that I had hit the lottery. There were so many girls and so little time."

Psalm 3:8 (KJV)

✓

Our Focus: We can only hope that what we have to offer will be shared with those in need. I use to think it was (only) for my benefit. Today, the greatest gift that I could receive is to have the right gift for another person.

✓

"I have been certain about the power of prayer. I now also accept the responsibility of my faith. There can be no faith without practice. I will be judge by twelve and not carried by six. That sentiment comes from a wise man who allowed HIS wife to edit the book you are now holding. They did a great job and she does wonderful work. Say a little prayer for them they are my friends. I love you guys-AMEN."

Psalm 84:26 (KJV)

✓

Our Focus: Let us seek to be witnesses of HIS word and HIS will.

✓

"To be understood I must understand others. We are all equal in the words of our forefathers. Let us honor that spirit more today to secure our foundation. Stop the violence. Share the love. Spread the peace."

Romans 1:16 (KJV)

✓

Our Focus: We have been given a great task by which the creator will be glorified. Let us do our best to reach our mark.

✓

"In the course of a year the harvest occurs in many places. I give a heartfelt thanks to my Maker for the breadth of HIS bounty. I am a true believer in the season of my blessings for they have come without disruption to my spirit. What your faith has delivered you from do not let your doubt bring you there again. Keep turning it over to HIM and you will in a better direction."

Isaiah 12:2 (KJV)

✓

Our Focus: we can make our lives fuller by giving credit where credit is due. Thank your GOD for the life you live; then, you can live it more abundantly.

Introspection: Week 26

We are a difficult culture to satisfy. In self-help we learn that satisfaction is contingent on awareness. I know that I am living in the solution when I can see someone in need and not look away. Then, I am practicing the truth of the program without reservation.

✓

"My toughest obstacle I have overcome. I am not in this battle alone. My faith is in HE who will supply the resources I need. My trust I put only in GOD. There is no shortcut or underpass to defeat the enemy. The competition is head to head. Now, I can play by my rules. I know who is in charge and who takes charge."

Psalm 149:4 (KJV)

✓

Our Focus: We have come to a crossroads. The challenge is to move forward.

✓

"When you live in the spirit there is no need to control its expression. For the spirit has a purpose. It is here to enhance your life by showing you how to live in the light. The journey is personal in its goal. Do not fear your faith will take you there."

Philippians 2:12 (KJV)

✓

Our Focus: We do good deeds to nurture our spirits. Let us nurture our spirit to do good deeds.

✓

"There is much to be thankful for in our daily lives. Our families we often take for granted. Throughout our lives Providence has revealed the importance of family. Family is to happiness as water is to life. Give your family your unending love in the time you have every day. They will be on your side no matter what."

Ephesians 3:15 (KJV)

✓

Our Focus: Remember one person does not make a family tree. Plant your seeds with care while you can still sample the fruit.

✓

"There are times when consequences dictate that there be a sort of punishment. In psychology, there are pros and cons on this subject. In my life it was not the sentence, but whom was going to render the sentence. My parents gave me stiffer time than I ever received in a courtroom. They were good parents whom knew how to correct their child. It was their duty."

Ecclesiastes 12:13 (KJV)

✓

Our Focus: My goals have been reset to be more feasible for me. I know that I can accomplish them in my lifetime as my GOD sees fit for me.

✓

"In this country there is more that could be done for those in need. Personally, I donate clothing, money, and food during the holidays and spring. If you have ever seen a homeless person when spring begins, you will be more inclined to surrender those prejudices. I pray every day for forgiveness."

Psalm 147:11 (KJV)

✓

Our Focus: Life offers many pleasures. Subsequently, there are some that come with a great price. Do not be afraid to play if you want to pay.

✓

"When you have answered the call to serve it is most determined by how you were called. Let the best come from your heart that you can offer. No servant ever goes without the help of the Creator. Serve well."

Joshua 8:1 (KJV)

✓

Our Focus: The family that prays together stays together.

✓

"Our justice system may never be what we desire it
to be. However, we all can contribute to improving it.
We ought to practice our civil rights and respond to the
jury notices. They are not advertisements. Do not take
the basic foundations of this system for granted. They
can be gone when you wake up."

Psalm 56:4 (KJV)

✓

Our Focus: We need to take the reins of this "horse
and buggy." No one can do it for us. Get out and get
involved. Let your voice be heard.

Introspection: Week 27

In our daily relations there is much to see that makes life matter. There is no room for grandiosity or arrogance. The more we resist such indulgences, the stronger our connection to the world beyond the here and now.

✓

"We hope that when the day of the LORD comes that HE will find faith on earth. Shamefully, we know that the issues we face diminish our belief in GOD. HE is rich in grace and mercy and doubt may be a natural part of the human experience. Do not resist the need to commune with HIM."

Luke 18:8 (KJV)

✓

Our Focus: we must draw the line to manage ourselves. Perhaps we will be released from the bondage of self-centeredness. To GOD be the glory.

✓

"For decades the argument over what the soul is
has been the topic on many believers' minds. The word
of GOD tells us that, when HE breathed the "breath
of life" that; man became a living soul. The entire
manifestation of oneself is the soul. Many years I spent
thinking the soul was some little invisible part of me
that could fly. That is just an example how the enemy
distorts the truth in GOD'S word. GOD made man a
living soul not; living with a soul."

Mark 4:40 (KJV)

✓

Our Focus: we have more responsibility to ourselves
than we would acknowledge. Cultivate your spirituality
and you will feel better.

✓

"Faith has a way of revealing to others the things we want to change about ourselves. When we can accept criticism then, we can claim to have humility. Such an asset will make service more attainable. Keep up the good work by moving on to the next level."

Romans 10:17 (KJV)

✓

Our Focus: There is a time and a place for everything. When you know that it is time, make sure you are in a good place.

✓

"I am in for the long haul of life. Through the prayers and hope of those that love me when I don't love myself. I have begun to live as though I want to live. The pursuit of pleasure no longer controls my behavior. The love of others has picked me up from despair. I have not seen love like this before I could tell anyone who I was."

Ephesians 1:18 (KJV)

✓

Our Focus: Do not harden yourselves to the power of love.

✓

"I am not the model citizen. However, I do obey the law because, that is the best way to remain free. My faith gives me the motivation to help others see the light. Employing my gifts demonstrates gratitude. I have a lot to give to anyone I may meet o any day. I have learned how to not derail my own blessings as a result of my human condition."

Romans 5:6 (KJV)

✓

Our Focus: We need confidence to be examples that others emulate. The glory is GOD'S, the work is ours. Be thankful for your part.

✓

"There are consequences for our actions whether good or bad. Sometimes we think that; we must pay the price for being right. That is debt we could never pay. When you close your mind you close your doors. That is the only thing that could close you out of your opportunity. An open mind is like the wheel. It did not exist until it was discovered."

2 Corinthians 5:17 (KJV)

✓

Our Focus: Each one teach one. We all share in the purpose of faith.

✓

"When we can show up at a friend's house and receive what we hoped for, we are glad we had trust. Our rationale for trust can be limited to what we can perceive. However, when you access the spiritual there is more giving than receiving. I think our only problem is that we know that we cannot have our way when it comes to receiving. Place your cares in HIS hands and let go."

Galatians 2:20 (KJV)

✓

Our Focus: Let our deeds for today be the testimony we give tomorrow. Hindsight is twenty-twenty. You can't get any better than that.

Introspection: Week 28

The most influential person in our lives may just be the one who tells us to do it our way. On the other hand, this same person may be the one who disciplines us. Choose carefully which way you go. We may gain more from the latter.

✓

"There were some preconceived ideas about women. I had some very positive examples of what a woman is. In my early youth I was somewhere out in left field. However, my dad *never* tied to tell me how a woman is. I respected him for that. I knew the woman I kept, my dad would not approve. My expectations have been exceeded."

1 Corinthians 11:7 (KJV)

✓

Our Focus: When I became a man, the gratitude for how I was raised sank in.

✓

"My adult life has been a quest for few things as important as wisdom. I have discovered that wisdom grows from learning about the mistakes of others. It is in the context of them making the mistakes again, it's in me making their mistakes. We are all in it together but, do we want to be?"

Proverbs 4:5 (KJV)

✓

Our Focus: By respecting others I have become someone others respect.

✓

"There is a growing movement of health consciousness. We are more attentive to our appearance and we critique our lifestyle daily. Proper eating and exercise will produce a more attractive self-image. When you get the priorities in order then you can educate yourself. Soon you will join us. Good luck!!!"

Psalm 19:7 (KJV)

✓

Our Focus: Be watchful of your likes and dislikes. Your motives may need some alteration. Sometimes boredom makes things seem not as they are. Monitor your feelings and thoughts.

✓

"In life it is necessary to give attention to details. I have learned this truth recently. My goal is to be an innovative force in my friends' thought processes. This will take time and effort. I love my friends with great passion for they have made my load light. Turn your challenge into a goal."

Acts 23:35 (KJV)

✓

Our Focus: How we perceive our environment will formulate how our perspective shape those surroundings. In other words, we do not want to back ourselves in a corner just to be overwhelmed by self-centeredness.

✓

"When we are experiencing discord there could be an underlying current of contempt. Experience gives us the knowledge of where reeling thoughts could lead. Make your plea to your confidant to get grounded. There is always a better response than one that comes out of panic. If you have spent the time to build trust then, let your relationship be the source of your comfort."

Acts 8:21 (KJV)

✓

Our Focus: Allow plenty of time for renewal by that which you hold close. Your place in their heart will always be there.

✓

"I have committed many sins. I use to think that sin was repetitive. That inexperience made it seem not so bad. Only the LORD can diminish sin. The joy comes when we realize that HE also forgives us of sin. I began to pray for my forgiveness to be transferable. I wanted to forgive those that had harmed me"

"Without HIM I would continue in my disobedience as it pertains to my human condition. I have seen the futile results of my self-reliant heart. I could not stop the things from happening that; were in GOD"S word. Humbly, I accepted that HE did not count e as an enemy buy; a child of HIS will. I came to the LORD by HIS word not mine."

Matthew 18:22 (KJV)

✓

Our Focus: We are bonded together through service. Yet, we exist separately from service. The LORD does hear each one of us.

✓

"On any given day there could be any number of family emergencies. My family rest a lot easier when I am healthy. My doctor gives me much hope however, none of it comes from above. Just imagine what HE could do for you. Do not just concentrate on who GOD is but see want HE can do for you. There is much release in that realization that GOD can do anything but let you down."

Matthew 16:24 (KJV)

✓

Our Focus: My place in life was taken. The enemy treated me like I was alone. GOD simply "tapped" my shoulder. Then, I knew HE was here and now.

✓

'Those were my first words as an employee. I was told what to say however, some things are revealed by thinking. Working showed me I could think for I while, my education showed me that others think about me. I would have never known CHRIST thought about me had I refused to think for myself."

Romans 1:3 (KJV)

✓

Our Focus: We can make a difference by teaching others how to be of service in order, to receive service. Yikes. This is a run on sentence. Needs rewrite. Consider "We make a difference by teaching others about service."

✓

"Becoming more like the man I was meant to be has inspired me. I love being an uncle, brother, and a brother-in-law. I wanted to be a father however, that dream is in the LORD'S hands. My whole world is in HIS hands."

Romans 1:5 (KJV)

✓

Our Focus: I have made my claim for my life. Now, I give it to the LORD and HE will provide.

✓

"We say that we need more time to get things in order. Yet, we are not specific about which things. However, all of us have the same time. We at time spear to make time for ourselves but, something always is put off till later. It passes the same way for us all. Make use of your time so that in time HE may make use of you. You have to be either cold or hot."

1 Thessalonians 4:16 (KJV)

✓

Our Focus: I have paid much attention to my thoughts. They have been inspired for the glory of GOD. When I do not want to listen to them is when I am running the show.

Introspection: Week 29

If we lay down to die than where we die will be where we lay. Put no hindrance on any man whom serves the LORD. HE knows who is HIS.

✓

"In the world today we work for the right to be self-sufficient. We could argue about what makes a person so diligent. On the other hand, we could say it is nothing but an illusion. Doesn't everybody need somebody? No matter how successful, all of us were given an opportunity then, we could make opportunities. There is no person who relies only on himself or herself. Keep working and soon the day of reckoning will come for you."

Matthew 27:40 (KJV)

✓

Our Focus: There is more to life than an exciting career. We ought to seize the opportunity to serve. It is the backbone of all the things we hold dear.

✓

Romans 12:23 says, "And be not conformed to this world: but be ye transformed by the renewing of your mind…" This scripture illustrates the importance of prayer in proper relation to GOD. We can improve with effort and faith. There is nothing that we need which GOD would keep from us. It is our responsibility to talk with GOD. HE is available outside of the church or any other house of worship."

Romans 12:2 (KJV)

✓

Our Focus: It has been my hope to see a change in the ideology of the church. That day is on the horizon. People are demanding it. Speak up.

✓

"My life lacked compassion. I had to give love in order to receive love or be given love. That principle has been a hallmark in my world. It has not failed me even when I do not feel love for myself. Sometimes, I am the hardest person to love when I need to love somebody. Compassion allows me to be tolerant of my own faults without criticizing myself to death. I seem to always feel love when I am willing to give love."

Ephesians 3:12 (KJV)

✓

Our Focus: We have done many acts of faith. We are called to reach even higher. Serving is not for the faint of heart; therefore, get in there for your self-respect.

✓

"I have made my life an example of obedience to my GOD. There was not much I could do when my mind caught up to my conscience. There were steep emotional changes taking place in my heart. I could no longer deny that I needed HIM.. It was going to take time to tell HIM all that I had to let go. My heart beats to the drums of empathy. There is no greater joy than making that human connection with someone like yourself."

Ephesians 2:10 (KJV)

✓

Our Focus: My colleagues confer much praise upon me. I, in turn, bestow the blessing upon my family and the gratitude to the LORD. Share the goodness.

✓

"All of us want to be confident about our decisions. In fact, children sometimes feel they can manage their own lives. We can empathize only because, we were once children who wanted it all too. However, our kids seem to need something more. Join the discussion for you may be able to shed some light on the situation. We would be forever grateful."

Psalm 71:1 (KJV)

✓

Our Focus: We have made progress with many issues surrounding our children. Do not drag your heels now. We still have some parenting to do.

✓

"We never know when but it happens to us all. Our health is failing. It may just be fatigue or exhaustion. Family and friends tell us to see our doctor. Use this time to strengthen your relationships. Do not allow yourself to become alienated. It is always nice to have loved ones around when you are under the weather."

John 5:24 (KJV)

✓

Our Focus: Take the time to visit your loved ones. You may be just what the doctor ordered. Your presence will be the best present that receive.

✓

"There is nothing that can raise school spirit such as the Homecoming. There are parties and everything social is happening. In my year, Homecoming meant the end of a decade of bad luck. We beat our long standing varsity football rival at home. We earned our right to graduate. The whole school contributed to that victory and it felt like they did. Young people stay in school."

2 Corinthians: 5:6 (KJV)

✓

Our Focus: Many of us have seen the light, but has the light been shown by many of us? Encourage one another to do your assignments, attend class, and graduate. You do not want to feel left out.

Introspection: Week 30

There is much in life to experience and enjoy. Develop your taste for the finer things carefully. Do not be overwhelmed by your emotions. They can get the best of you if you are careless. Life is meant to progress with us, not against us, then act with confidence.

✓

"I have made a host of friends that love me dearly. I am doing something right and I love them too. My parents taught how to listen when someone is talking to me. Now, I do much more listening than talking because, when I talk, others listen."

Psalm 18:32 (KJV)

✓

Our Focus: The day will come when the people whom (who or that) love us will lean on us. Take stock of that day, for such a responsibility is priceless.

✓

"We have been given many blessings. I would imagine that there are some passing by right now. Count your blessings and your blessings will count. Whatever else matters the "Willing Power" has it. Do not get in a frenzy about the things you cannot control. Put your trust in prayer, then GOD, and finally in your understanding. HE gave us our brains to think with not just to fill us up."

Psalm 18:32 (KJV)

✓

Our Focus: There are some aspects of life that require our immediate attention. However, we do at times have to wait for cooler heads to proceed.

✓

"People are a wonderful part of being connected to life. However, life requires that: for us to be content we must contribute. All I have to give is hope for it is the foundation of what I have accomplished. If there is anything that comes from what I do that helps you that is a divine intervention neither you nor I can take the credit for. My GOD comes and when HE does great things occur."

Psalm 109:104 (KJV)

✓

Our Focus: Today, let there be nothing keeping you back from meeting the day's challenges. It is your destiny to shine.

✓

"I would be hard press to discuss visions and dreams with no thought of their psychiatric implications. Historically, they have been the loophole in the realm of treatment at times, they were the motivation of authorities' to commit horrendous violations of patients' rights. I would suggest talking to someone who has similar beliefs you do to help you understand them. If you feel they are just a part of sleep then do not waste time when there are many other things to occupy your attention. Some things about life will not ever make sense to us."

Psalm 31:12 (KJV)

✓

Our Focus: We all have at one time or another needed to "dump" with a friend or family member. If you can carry a load you can release it.

✓

"Many of the ideas I had about weakness did not make sense in real life. They proved to be ideas that were survival skills on the streets. However, just because I have changed does not mean the streets have. Sometime trouble will find you when you are not looking for it. There are people who think that they are entitled to make life miserable for others. Do not be a part of the problem that was my weakness."

2 Corinthians 13:4 (KJV)

✓

Our Focus: Make today the last day that you think is the last day of your life.

✓

"Money does make us happy when we have it and when we get it. In this world there are many opinions about the purpose of money. We all know what money has to do with wealth. I stop being money hungry because I have wealth. The desire to have money is still a priority because, I have to eat, pay taxes, and get healthcare. Somehow my needs are met and I can go to a movie now and then. I do not want to be always on the stroll for money but; I do have to live. Can I get a witness?"

Proverbs 19:4 (KJV)

✓

Our Focus: I have more time to share with others. It is not what I have that matters – It's me. GOD is good all the time and all the time GOD is good. That was the mantra of my church home.

✓

"Living has brought me gratitude and wisdom. I cannot think of any two principles that complement each other more. I do not know which happened first but; they are both indispensable when you serve the GOD of your understanding. For me they are part of the good life. I could not have succeeded without them."

Proverbs 16:16 (KJV)

✓

Our Focus: Let us make our lives a testimony to the wisdom we have gained.

Introspection Week 31

I have the proper way to stay motivated. All my relationships are in the right perspective. There is no one who tries to make me feel less than. However, I am less than worried about who I am. My hope and desire rests the hands of HE who made me- I need not be afraid.

✓

"If we are careless about our choices we may face dire consequences. Sometimes I seek a confidant before making a choice or decision. It is a relief to not have to know everything. Sometimes two heads are better than one."

2 Corinthians 12:14 (KJV)

✓

Our Focus: Be ready to accept responsibility for your actions. It does not necessarily mean something has gone wrong.

✓

"Some days life will go our way however, more than not we will have to compromise. There are times when pother people take priority over us. I know that my nephew is more of a priority to my brother than I am. He is only two years old. At that age, children need around the clock care. Therefore, there are days I do not eat because, I do not have the means to secure a meal. I have learned that eating is a privilege in the world today. On other day I can do like anyone else and negotiate my way into a meal. Relax, it can be a real pleasure working with others."

James 3:17 (KJV)

✓

Our Focus: We can start our day over whenever we need to.

✓

"When we become mature there is a part of us which realizes our needs are different than our wants. The way satisfy that desire to splurge or play it close lies in our free will. When I began to support myself I forgot all about those finer things I wanted. I was happy to eat every day. That does not mean I had three meals a day. In fact, today I do not have three meals a day. I finally got it. I want to be able to meet my needs. The lessons of life are not absent from the classroom just look at the writing on the board and follow the instructions. The reason that I go hungry is because of some wrong choices I made. GOD is not punishing me I am not that familiar with GOD. Yet, I know that I have it better than much of the world."

Isaiah 55:1 (KJV)

✓

Our Focus: I have been able to attain a measure of satisfaction by keeping an open mind. Be willing to work for what you want. In some cases you have to be ready to lay down your life to keep what is yours.

✓

"We can make a better life by making a life better for us. Do not get stuck on the endless nerve pounding competition of the "rat race" in this life. All that we truly value does not wear a price tag. If you look carefully you will see the value of things is only in how they make us feel. The lift is temporary. Choose wisely what you will do."

Luke 1:50 (KJV)

✓

Our Focus: We have come to a crossroads in our lives. The only way we will go is the way we choose. No one makes that choice for us.

✓

"There are many attributes a man can have but, are they qualities only of a man? I do not claim to know why people like me. In fact, it is really none of my business. My goal is to treat people with respect. My duty is to be ready to serve. Humbly I can tell you that; I cannot get us back into the garden but, we will eat. (LOL) You can have the message without shooting the messenger."

Deuteronomy 6:5 (KJV)

✓

Our Focus: It is our will that we be given the resources to make a difference. The help we offer does matter. Our sweat- GOD'S work

✓

"I have labored for a specific purpose. I want to encourage others to work on their dreams. Sometimes the idle mind is tapped by a power of a more positive nature-our conscience. We must be ready to move into action. You want to be in position to receive grace. The LORD will not force HIS goodness on us yet, all we have to do is ask that we be given it. Prayers go up as do praises and both deliver us from ruin."

Jeremiah 31:3 (KJV)

✓

Our Focus: I did not look for a way out of trouble, for only another person can show me the way out. That miracle is of a sacred covenant for the blessing of many. I only hope to receive in order to give.

✓

"I have seen copies of some very special paintings. It heightened my appreciation of hard work and dedication. I have priorities today that keep me living responsibly. The life that is my masterpiece has been given to me by a power greater than I. I am certain that it is the right power."

Psalm 36:9 (KJV)

✓

Our Focus: My path has many bends and curves, yet I do not fall or stumble. I pause and that gives me the clarity of mind to think again. Thinking is a privilege that you should not deny yourself.

Introspection: Week 32

My passion is for service to my GOD. There I find myself and the love only that power can give. GOD gives only that which is in human terms "perfect". I do not try to match HIS love. My prayer is to reciprocate to others. I pray that your seeking brings you peace.

✓

"This line use to stir up negative images that made me uncomfortable. Then I thought to myself that some things already come in pieces. My life came in pieces for which I had to find the directions. When I started this life I needed GOD. It did not grow on me like my appetite for a meal. It was a relief to know that the darkness which affected my life did not shatter it into pieces. I did not get protection I was protected by my GOD. HE came with life I did not pick HIM out of a line-up."

Psalm 91:16 (KJV)

✓

Our Focus: There are few words that stir me like the word- gratitude. It takes many emotions to express it to someone I know. It is an intrinsic value that I do not deny.

✓

"The challenge of life is to determine do you want more than this. It is a basic consequence of being born. As we grow, it is usually us who makes the fuss over us. There is s nothing shameful for we should treat ourselves good. The will to live is not something that is guaranteed. Taking lives for granted is not a quality of the Creator."

John 3:36 (KJV)

✓

Our Focus: We have made many mistakes in our judgment. Grace forbids our mistakes making us. There is always hope.

✓

"There will be many days to live end enjoy the simple pleasures of life. It is wise to prepare for that time in order that we may be content. If we are lucky we will be sharing those days with others. Such a blessing I hope will not pass me by. It is a great way to break bread with those you are raveling this road with."

John 1:9 (KJV)

✓

Our Focus: I want to be in the process of life with full steam ahead. Waves do not make me sea sick. The strong arm of the LORD keeps me buoyant.

✓

"Making our lives prosperous requires commitment. We also must possess a degree of courage. Do not be afraid to invest in yourself. You are your most valued commodity. The game begins and ends with you and your actions. There is no glory in letting yourself go for a momentary dose of pleasure."

Psalm 100:4 (KJV)

✓

Our Focus: Let us give credit where credit is due. Thank you LORD for your grace and mercy. We have all we need when it comes to serving.

✓

"In this context, we are concerned about responsibility for our actions towards others and ourselves. We want to demonstrate our gratitude for what we been given. The world is changing rapidly in other words, there is very little that our loved ones do not know about us. Therefore, let us pray with an open and humble heart. The LORD loves a cheerful giver let that be your goal for today."

Philippians 4:6 (KJV)

Our Focus: When I awake each morning I am fully aware that it requires more than an alarm clock. In addition, I am full of gratitude.

✓

"My family and I have witnessed many days of uncertainty. Until we stopped hardening our hearts we believed it was just "bad luck". Our new attitude is one that was given by a greater power than us. In this life we have much to gain when we resist the temptation to live above the law. This shift comes from *surrendering* to the will of GOD. We have different ideas about GOD but not what HE can do. Today, we trust in that power with our whole hearts."

Psalm 41:1 (KJV)

✓

Our Focus: I like to give flowers to those I love. However, my loved ones do not seem to catch on. I would love to receive flowers. Quiet, that is a secret.

✓

"Living alone makes it almost impossible for me to be happy. I needed to allow people to get to know me. Sharing my life gave me strength to ask for HIS strength. I was given an understanding that I did not have before. Now, I am strong when I feel weak. I can speak when there are no words. I have a surge in my step that carries me on the clouds of life. My body feels like it has been caressed by the hands of who I most desire. The LORD withholds no joy to convince those HE finds pleasure in."

Exodus 15:2 (KJV)

Our Focus: I try to be an example for my nieces' every day. That is the greatest gift I can give. I will be in the spirit when I am called on by love.

✓

"Economics never interested me much. I always wanted to understand the reason behind certain motivations. There was nothing noble about it perhaps, I would get smarter. However, I could not satisfy all my curiosity. I understood that there were limits. I had to shift my focus. I learned that what I needed to know I would. There are times when I want something for nothing."

Psalm 46:1 (KJV)

✓

Our Focus: Today, life gives us many chances to get ahead. Savvy minded professionals brave the markets while everyday ay workers are more confident about bonds and savings. Either way, take stock, period. Then, "Now…" now you are on call.

September 6   Feed the spirit

"Our spirituality needs to be sustained. I challenge you to complete a more nurturing task than helping someone in need. On the way to do your good deed try not to tell anyone. No man can ever reward you for your sacrifice. The glory is all GOD'S but the memory is yours. Look to the LORD for your gifts that way you know there will not be anything you cannot handle."

Romans 1:11 (KJV)

Our Focus: Be fair to your associates. They are friends without the label.

✓

"I Corinthians 10:3 says, "And did all eat the same spiritual meat." When someone cares enough to share the right information, who are we to add and subtract from it. Turn away from gossip and state the facts. Thus far, you have not contemplated any gossip please; keep reading for there is more about you."

"The people who can continue have started to get some insight to how we got here.. It is a major change to see yourself doing this work in order to help someone else be heard. I applaud you for your vision. Whoever helped you to see gave you a gift that will make you and your family proud. Do not regret it."

I Corinthians 10:3 (KJV)

✓

Our Focus: At the end of the day we ought to be comfortable enough to retire. Leave office issues at the place where they belong. After all, you have the right not to be perfect.

Introspection: Week 33

I am in the process of continuing my education. My goal is to be forthright about what works and how it works. Reasons have always been GOD'S business. I am not being a player. I am simply playing a role model to help those who are coming of age. I use to be young too.

✓

"We make decisions based on our understanding of a situation. It would be great to know all there is to consider for every decision. When we ask for help there has to be some expectation on the outcome. We are all doing the best we can to perform our duties while considering who benefits. Self-respect means that we do not perform or underperform our jobs at the cost of the very things we value most- friends and family. Think less and listen more."

Psalm 31:12 (KJV)

✓

Our Focus: The measure of our progress is not always in dollars and cents. Sometimes it is a matter of giving and receiving.

✓

"The best course of action is the majority rule. I would imagine so in government however, a family decision is not always democratic. When my dad made a decision that was the ruling. Only mom could contest it but she learned early in our history to choose her battles. Which meant, we were not going to get everything we wanted. I was the one who doubted his judgment. I lost some good play time."

Colossians 1:9 (KJV)

✓

Our Focus: My years at home were a bittersweet time. However, my conscience tells me I can make anything better simply by understanding.

✓

"The opportunity to advance can come before you are prepared properly. There is no guessing how the break will be presented. My best defense is an earnest offense- prayer works. By relying upon HIS word I can face the truth. There are times I want to be in the driver's seat again. I have long memory about my efforts at self-reliance. I am glad that I can ask for help."

Psalm 37:3 (KJV)

✓

Our Focus: HE will make believers out of non-believers and non-believers out of believers. It is wise to yield to the will of the LORD for therein lies peace.

✓

"A few years ago today, I knew that prayer made a difference. I have not forgotten how scared I was. The world was changed by the acts of a group of men whom hated another group of men. It was a tragedy that shocked the cultural foundation of this country. Yet, there were people trying to go about like business as usual. The world as we knew it ended September 11, 2001 at 8:47AM. We can make or break our future."

Psalm 31:165 (KJV)

✓

Our Focus: The feelings may never go away. The memories will last for our sakes to serve as a reminder that we are vulnerable to those who hate.

✓

'It is important to teach your children right and wrong. They will thank you for it someday. When I left home, I was very happy my parents did what they could. I had nothing but the clothes on my back. In fact, I did not have any skills to support myself on either. I had a substance problem that was not going to allow me to let my parents support while I try abstinence. So, I took responsibility for my life. My errors did not follow me wherever I went. My chances were slim to none but, I took them for the good of all concerned."

Acts 2:38 (KJV)

✓

Our Focus: My life today is the best life I have ever had. I may be poor but I have control of my body again as well as my mind. My hope comes from a greater power than I

✓

"There are many colors in the world. Sometimes we describe each other by color. It is convenient for us. Colors are used for other things than people. Show your colors with pride and respect the colors of others. There is a commonality amongst us that reaches beyond the colors we use. Colors are not bad but, people do some bad things in the name of colors. Respect is the lesson here take it with you wherever you go and you will continue to respect yourself."

Psalm 51:10 (KJV)

✓

Our Focus: We are in the midst of a great event. Today, we can make a difference in someone's day. Imagine your act of kindness repeated.

✓

"I think part of the attraction of shopping is the freedom to get something for nothing. Some stores have mastered this concept. However, you must inquire about the policy. You must have certain standards that the stores state in their policy. It is no guarantee but; people look for these conditions every day. You may experience that rush again. Give it your best shot."

1 Timothy 5:18 (KJV)

✓

Our Focus: Any privilege that is abused gets rescinded. Be smart- leave the game to the kids. You will come out better in the long run.

Introspection: Week 34

There are always people who take you at your word. I am fortunate enough to have two such people in my circle. They have their own way of reaching me unlike anyone else. They are not afraid to tell me the truth. These people belong on my gratitude list – Thank you.

✓

"I have made many people a lot of money. I learned my lesson then. Principles build on one another. I still work like my life depends on it. It seems as though there are a lot of confused people in the world. Some people get rich while the majority of us struggle to make the rent and pay the insurance. How do we make it less radical? Who controls the distribution of the wealth? There are many questions that all lead to more questions. This is not about asking the right question when no one really seems to know. In my opinion we have too many chiefs and not enough tribesman."

Matthew 10:31 (KJV)

✓

Our Focus: I have seen my share of tragedy. I like being around my friends when they are thriving. I seek them when they are down. Either way they are mine.

✓

'Making plans for your life is a way to improve the odds of being successful. Therefore, do not plan haphazardly. Your road to success has fellow travelers. They will try emulate you as you improve your situation. Remember, no man is an island. Wherever you receive your strength from make sure it is a natural origin. Do not fall for that counterfeit strength of fast money and fast results. Anything worth having takes time in fact, it takes longer than you are willing to wait."

Ecclesiastes 1:18 (KJV)

✓

Our Focus: Give yourself the benefit of the doubt. There are many ways to contribute to society that yield sizeable returns. You do not have to be altruistic.

✓

"I have been fortunate in my attempt to return to college. The work load was great and the standards high. The primary factor affecting my work was willingness. I had it and I used it to be the best I could. There was nothing that I did not do to maximize the results of my sacrifice. I prayed every day without missing a day. I was challenged by the objective of my classes which was to make me a capable professional that could perform his duties in compliance with the ethics and quality of the field of study. My future was here and now in fact, I thought that I had missed the boat. As a result of my dedication and consistency I was honored by my educators for my academics. This was going to be an alternative to the original plan. I stood ready to serve."

Job 28:28 (KJV)

✓

Our Focus: We can make or break an opportunity. You have to really dig deep,

✓

"Here and now there is much conflict about a lot of concerns people share. No one wants to be seen as an instigator. War is not the only event that can boost the economy. In order for us to go in a different direction we need to get out to be heard. The people who represent us will not consider alternatives when there is no one supporting them. Remember, this is a government by the people, for the people, and of the people. It takes work to make those in charge listen to what we have to say. Make sure your voice is heard as high as it can go. Don't give up the fight."

Matthew 11:12 (KJV)

✓

Our Focus: Keep your focus on promoting peace and non-violence. We will build and HE will come.

✓

"There is much to say about empathy. In this life, we would do well to learn how to practice it with everyone. This quality has made my life richer and more rewarding. I have peace when I try to understand where you are coming from without assuming I know before I know. We can all be more cohesive with our environment when we extend ourselves to our neighbors. Do yourself a favor and learn how to speak with your heart and just your head."

Proverbs 16:22 (KJV)

✓

Our focus: Do the right thing for the right reason and the right reason will be the right thing. It is all in your mind. Do not waste it on strife.

✓

"I have had two best friends in my life. Today, both are still my friends. They will I believe, always be my friends. I realize there are things about me I want to change. Both my friends tell me what is true for they are genuine. I am glad that I did not have to choose. I want to honor their loyalty by being the most authentic person I can. They have never held back what I needed to hear. Friends to the end."

John 7:28 (KJV)

✓

Our Focus: We can make a good relationship better when we amend our behavior. I would not want to continue offending those I love.

✓

"I am appreciative to my family for their support. We have become a closer unit over time. They; look to me for advice and credibility. We encourage each other to always do our best. Each of us can lead but, none of us are followers. We live lives of obedience to the word of the LORD."

Acts 9:15 (KJV)

✓

Our Focus: My family time is precious to me. It means more to me than gold. I would lay down my life for them. They would remember me.

Introspection: Week 35

There is more time to bring about changes that will help all of us to be more compassionate. The meaning of life will not be found in a winning ticket. Instead, look into the heart of someone who has accepted the change in his or her life with a smile.

✓

"Our attitudes are generally the thing in us that keeps us stuck in life. When we are isolated there is not much happening. We tend to get bored easily. Break the cycle by taking a walk or go visit a friend. That is better than being lonely. You have the answers in your hand. Pause- then think about what you lie to do. Tough times do not have to be the way you live your life. Make your day as exciting as you want it."

Psalm 41:1 (KJV)

✓

Our Focus: My best day smoking is less than my worse day not smoking. The cigarette is not my master anymore.

✓

"There ae many indicators for when we are out of balance. The challenges we face daily are enough to make us think twice. That is a good tool for us to use regularly. We will make less mistakes over again when we think twice. Be prepared for whatever happens."

Mark 4:37 (KJV)

✓

Our focus: I have restored my reputation. What I have learned is: do not try to please everybody all the time. All I need to do is be willing to serve.

✓

"I had to figure out how to make my life better. My family, friends, and lovers all wanted to see it change. I do not like the way not being trusted feel s. I had to earn back the trust that I violated. It was going to be a long road. You do not appreciate some things until they are gone. Now, I love life and life is full of love for us all. My family has come back to me and I don't ever want to have to let them go again."

Exodus 15:2 (KJV)

✓

Our Focus: We cannot worry about who i(does instead of is) who does not play by the rules. When you know better you do better.

✓

"Sometimes we can see only what we want. When we become close-minded, pause for a moment. In that instant you can take a new perspective that will lead to a more promising outcome for you. Let the shift be your answer work for it- No fear."

Isaiah 52:10 (KJV)

✓

Our Focus: together we can make a world of difference in a world of indifference.

✓

"For me, telling others about my life is futile when I do not include the part GOD played in it. I could not have changed anything without prayer. I do not have the power I though I did. It is scary to be in trouble and realize that truth then. All I could do was get to the point of failure of self. Then, I hung my head in defeat and humiliation was all I knew. No one wanted me around but the LORD yet, that bridge was burned too. HE promised he would never forsake me but; I did not find that promise until it happened."

Psalm 100:2 (KJV)

✓

Our Focus: The truth about your life is sacred. Guard it carefully for the enemy will desire it. Do not sell your birthright for any price or pleasure. It is not real.

✓

"I use to get confused when it came to pride. Is it good or a sin? I still do not know but, I have faith all will be well. Therefore, I tell my nieces that I am proud of them. It feels almost like saying I love you. In there lies the difference when I can say I love you that is the pride we can show. There must be a different implication for the unwanted pride. I can trust my feelings towards my nieces."

Philippians 4:6 (KJV)

✓

Our Focus: The good life requires a liberal dose of courage. You never know what will get it started. It can come from almost anywhere.

✓

"When we get older we begin to learn a whole new set of manners. I like manners for they keep life civil. They saved me from some beatings too. The new manners can be just as effective. You do not know until you try. Let your conscience be your guide and you will be amazed at the results. Our parents knew what they were doing when they taught us how to respect people."

"If we all went around just doing anything we pleased this world would have been gone many years ago. Proper etiquette is one of the hallmarks of those who live the good life. I never doubted the benefits of demonstrating my manners. In fact, I knew they were important because, my dad honored them. I don't understand what their importance is then again, I do not need to."

Hebrews 11:6 (KJV)

✓

Our Focus: we have been in the process of a tumultuous change. Basically, I believe people are good and we are just self- centered.

Introspection: Week 36

Historically, we have been persuaded by the charisma of men who could speak to our greater purpose. They tantalized our feelings and gave us the emotions we share. Let us keep listening for the word will come whether we are ready or not ready. We cannot afford to miss our great calling.

"I have been pursuing knowledge for all my adult life. I have seen places I would rather forget. However, I am told that my experiences may be a light for someone else. Who am I to doubt the grace and mercy of GOD?"

2 Samuel 22:33 (KJV)

Our Focus: There are people who gladly share their wisdom to uplift others. I am my brother's keeper. Man up when you are called.

September 30   How bad do you want it?

✓

"I learned early that when you want something g you have to work for it. It is by the power of Providence that I breathe today. The enemy had me in its grip. GOD did not break the grip, HE broke its curse. No one else can do what He did. Now, the enemy does not even want his greatest weapon. He may as well throw it out."

Haggai 2:7 (KJV)

✓

Our Focus: There is passion in my spirit for the chance to serve. I know no better way to thank HIM. I look forward to seeing you there like me.

Holiday or Holiday Season

Our celebrations give us much pleasure and satisfaction. I have come to enjoy celebrating with family and friends. There are those of us who do not anticipate celebrating(period)Start new sentence with In fact...) in fact, we seem to ponder the meaning of the holidays. Historically, cultures around the world have set aside certain days as a time for remembrance and festival. These days are the highlight of their social activity for the calendar year. In this country we have holidays and then we have the holiday season. It appears that the holiday season is ambiguous for some of us (comma) specifically, those who contemplate the meaning of the holiday season. These same factions of the population seem to put a damper on the mood of the holiday season.

Holiday is a word comprised of two words- "holy" and "day". When these terms were combined into the word holiday, the secular constituency (put at the time in parenthesis)(at the time), wanted to keep both versions of the terminology. A holiday was seen as having a religious connotation and a social impact. People observed these days with fellow believers and family. There was an emphasis on conforming to the tradition of the holiday implications. These observances began to come together in the fabric of our nation and in Europe.

OK. There is no transition here, making this part very muddled. I WILL PUT IN MY SUGGESTIONS:

All sorts of idea, notions, and 0precepts were derived from making holidays more memorable each year. It is amazing how the ancestors were able to consistently recognize these days. I imagine they had conversations much the same way we have them today. In fact, I would not be surprised to note that they tackle some of the very same issues we deal with today. Children were able to enjoy the holidays with their parents and siblings. Subsequently, the church seemed to prosper from its organized status in the minds of the families that attended. They unanimously supported or favored the religious dynamic of the holiday season. They encouraged families to attend service and gave the youth special assignments. The children were given poems from the Bible to memorize in order to recite them at the service in front of the congregation. I would suspect the church wanted to gain control over its members

For almost three centuries the church sought to capitalize its power through the institution of its teachings while monitoring the behavior of its congregations. However, some of the followers began to inquire with others about a relatively obscure school of thought called "spirituality." What made it so compelling was the lack of a universally accepted definition for the term during the rise of the church. In the passing years there would be much debate and political influence on the public to define and demonstrate spiritual ability. There were some activist who made it known that virtually all religious teachings were intertwined with some form of spirituality. The church proposed that their teachings were founded on their traditions and a very popular version of GOD'S word called The "Holy Bible". The hierarchy of the church would soon find their way to detach from those that promoted a spiritual origin of the churches' ideology.

According to WA Ayman, the traditional meaning of the term spirituality is a process of re-formation which aims to recover the original shape of ma, the image of GOD. To accomplish this, the reformation is oriented at a mold, which represents the original shape. The dissenters of the early church wanted to dispel the myths connected to the dogma they were indoctrinated into. In fact, these same groups were able to trace the impact of spirituality to almost three hundred years before its emergence during the fifth century. These groups of believers did not want to eradicate the religious influence. Notwithstanding, they wanted to make certain their voices were hears above all the rhetoric. They continued to celebrate their holiday season, though some were merely focused on the social context. The first day of a holiday season is when the celebrating truly begins.

October

The first of the holiday season is Halloween. Halloween originated with the ancient Celtic festival called Samhain (Sam-hi). This festival was depicted as a time when the people lighted bonfires and adorned costumes to fend off wayward spirits. These spirits were thought to be the citizens who had died prior to the time of the festival. In addition, the observers would put snacks and drinks on their stoops, for they believed that the ghost were hungry. The Celts lived approximately two thousand years ago. They settled in Ireland, UK, and northern France. They were staunch supporters of their innate human right to have a relationship with GOD. During this eighth century scenario, the Christian church changed Samhain into All Saints Day. The Church went on to acknowledge intangible entities.

The young people were inclined to practice a form of alms called souling. Souling is when a group of parishioners come together to entertain folks in their homes in exchange for donations and contributions. They would then distribute the bounty to those in need without regard to their own lacking of supplies. The young people believed their souling practices as vital to the functioning of the church and the community. However, the church frowned on the generosity of the young people, thinking such a thing ought to benefit the members more than non-members. This practiced continued until it was revised in the mid nineteenth century.

In the mid-1950's Halloween became more family centered, than the work child oriented event. Surprisingly, it is the second most commercialized holiday superseded only by Christmas. We assign candy, sweets, and costumes to our celebration of Halloween. It has been like that for years. Unfortunately, there is a darker side to Halloween. Some people use it to exploit others who are unaware of the damage being imposed on their lives. It is upsetting to be aware of the maleficence some people harbor towards others. It has nothing to do with the holiday spirit. Subsequently, the answer as to the meaning of the holiday season may not be found in the celebration of Halloween. Let us look to the next date on the calendar in the holiday season...

November

This day, Thanksgiving, brings up many notions to all people. Some choose to be ultra-cautious about their behavior. It does matter what we do on Thanksgiving. Yet, some people think anything goes.(We have some personal and universal reasons for observing holidays. Historically, Thanksgiving implies that we as a nation do welcome alternatives to traditional core values that foster family celebrations. As a result, this holiday is one of the most anticipated days on the calendar.

Thanksgiving has always been a time for people to be more nostalgic in their observances. We are flooded with images of feasting and riches. Some of us even exchange gratuities and forget-me-nots. Thanksgiving brings a more personal relationship to the holiday season.

In 1621, the Plymouth colonists and Wampanoag Indians shared an autumn harvest feast acknowledged as one of the first Thanksgiving feast (ADD 'EVER') celebrated. These pioneers were not concerned with cultural or civic differences. They were focused on establishing a distinct level of communication between the two disparate groups. The Indians showed the colonists how to farm while preserving the land. The

Thanksgiving Day event was a time where they could honor those who were most instrumental in their survival.

The colonists were strangers in a foreign land. At that time there was no "melting pot". Each culture was responsible for its own survival. However, they could see how cooperation. Together, they could survive the conditions that challenged them in this newly discovered territory. The colonists were positioned to become an influence on the inhabitants of this land. The Indians were in need of certain technologies or instruments that the colonists possessed. It would prove to be a sensitive agreement that provides common ground. For example, the colonists knew how to navigate the seas. Such knowledge impressed the Wampanoag people because they were aware of the resources that the seas held. Also, they knew that the weather and other environmental factors were affected by the seas. They were accustomed to land travel, sea travel could prove to be necessary.

Thanksgiving is a worldwide recognized holiday. Its basic premise has stayed the same since it became a national holiday. Generations have marveled at the meals served on this day. Many households will serve their turkeys and cranberry sauce to all those who have waited patiently to taste their first bite of those meals prepared maybe with love. The dinner is preceded by a round of testimonials in which each person tells what they are thankful for, followed by a grace given by the eldest member of the family. It is a time where we who are blessed remember those less fortunate as our way of honoring the ONE whom made this all possible. Personally, this is my favorite day of the holiday season. It was when I was a kid too. Everyone was included on Thanksgiving and everything was for everyone. The holiday season culminates in the next day on the calendar.

December

Each year 30-35 million real Christmas trees are sold in the United States. There are twenty one thousand Christmas tree growers in the United States. No other holiday season day inspires such indulgence. We all know that the tree is an attraction for the children. This attraction goes all the way back to the seventeenth century. Children seem to think there is something magical about the tree. We know that children have always wondered what they would receive on Christmas. The baby JESUS was the first recipient of Christmas. As has been noted, HE received presents from the three kings who traveled across the dessert to honor HIM. There has been little modified about Christmas since that first Christmas.

In June of 1870, in fact June 26, 1870(c0mma) Christmas was declared a federal holiday. This holiday had religious as well as social manifestations. The Christian church scheduled services while,(no comma) communities planned gatherings and prepared snacks for citizens. The first eggnog made in the United States was consumed in Captain John Smith's 1607 Jamestown settlement. These celebrants were moved by the outpouring of support for their holiday acknowledgement. Christmas is and always will be the national day for giving. Yes, the eggnog was not altered, enjoyed just as it was served-cold. Finally, we will witness the close of the holiday season along with its jubilation and fanfare.

Cultures around the world have been celebrating New Years at least for a millennium. In society today, festivities begin on December 31st, the last day of the Gregorian calendar. These celebrations are the hallmarks for American culture, yet their origin came from overseas. Babylonians practiced a massive religious festival called Akitu derived from the Schelerian word for barley. They performed a different festival on each of its eleven days. Akitu celebrated the mythical victory of Marduk over Tiamat, the sea goddess. It was during this time a new king was crowned. (OK YOU NEED TO REWRITE THE NEXT SENTENCE TO MAKE SENSE. TRY : THE BEGINNING OF A NEW REGIME IMPACTED THE WORLD VIEW IN DIFFERENT WAYS { The beginning of a new regime impacted the civilizations of the world in different ways. Many Americans traveled to demonstrate their belief in the ideology of other cultures. The holiday season made a stage in the world for all who have other beliefs to share them with those who will listen. The holiday season will continue to inspire the socialization of our people in combination with the evolution of spirituality.

Finally, let the joy and ambiguity of the holiday season allow you to identify and personalize the meaning of the season. That is the beauty of this time of year. We can honor our own meaning of the holiday season. No one can tell you that what you know is wrong. Your family and friends will, more than not, be willing to share in your interpretation of this blessed observance. Be willing to share the wonderment with a child. The wonderment of our ancestors. Be willing to have a wonderful life!!!!

Have a wonderful life!!!

HOPE

"I have experienced the miracle of hope. It can make what is old seem new, what is broke seem better, and what is bad seem good. Whatever the struggle is let hope be what makes the difference. You are better off with some hope than without any. It will save the day. For a long time I had no hope subsequently, there was no connection or awareness of a power that could help me have the type of life I wanted. In addition, the people I saw living a life like I wanted did not all have hope. Some of them were simply very industrious. Those that did show hope told me they would not want it any other way. Miracles do happen to us all."

NOTES

NOTES

NOTES

Sources

1. http:// www.history.com/ topics/holidays, 2014-
   <u>Holidays- facts, meanings, impact</u>

2. http:// www.adha.com/true meaning/holiday/
   season,2009-<u>The true meaning of the holiday
   season</u>

3. <u>Webster's Basic Dictionary</u>, 2010, Minerva
   Books- New York

4. http://www.jeffbaldridge.com/blog/what
   is-the-meaning-of-the-holidays-for-you,
   2012-Baldridge, J., Dr.